INSIDE MAVERICK'S

Photography by Doug Acton
Edited by Bruce Jenkins and Grant Washburn
Introduction by Richard Schmidt

INSIDE MAVERICK'S
PORTRAIT OF A MONSTER WAVE

CHRONICLE BOOKS
SAN FRANCISCO

Library of Congress Cataloging-in-Publication Data:

Inside Maverick's : portrait of a monster wave / edited by Bruce
Jenkins and Grant Washburn ; photographs by Doug Acton ;
introduction by Richard Schmidt.

p. cm.

ISBN-10: 0-8118-5121-4
ISBN-13: 978-0-8118-5121-3

1. Surfing—United States—History.
2. Surfing—California—Half Moon Bay—History.
3. Surfers—United States. I. Jenkins, Bruce, 1948- II. Washburn, Grant.

GV840.S8I54 2006
797.3'20973—dc22
2006002982

Manufactured in China

Designed by Jeff Canham

Distributed in Canada by Raincoast Books
9050 Shaughnessy Street
Vancouver, British Columbia V6P 6E5

10 9 8 7 6 5 4 3 2 1

Chronicle Books LLC
85 Second Street
San Francisco, California 94105

www.chroniclebooks.com

In memory of Jay Moriarity, the embodiment of stoke.
Thanks for showing us the way.

TABLE OF CONTENTS

FOREWORD

GRANT WASHBURN

He paddled for the first wave of the set, and missed it. It had been a spectacular session up to that moment, loaded with thrilling rides, but suddenly things had changed. It was Halloween 1992, one of the biggest days ever ridden, and the fun was over.

We'd talked many times about the mistake no one wanted to make at Maverick's, and my buddy had just made it. I looked toward the horizon as John Raymond struggled to turn his 10'6" around. It was too late. The set was big, many towering walls of water, all bearing down on the impact zone and my friend. There was no way to help, nothing to do but watch as he prepared for his ultimate nightmare.

The pit of my stomach dropped when the next wave sucked out in front of him. It felt like I was in there myself. I felt his pain and I saw his terror. There would be no escape, just the question of whether he could survive.

Ditching his board as the first wave reared over him, he got under it and eventually surfaced, but the wave sucked him deep into the maelstrom. The turmoil was horrendous as he fought to stay near the surface. Whirlpools of foam spun him down before the next wave arrived, and it was bigger than the last. He popped up again, his chin barely breaking the surface as he gasped for a breath, and the next heaving barrel was coming down right on top of him. He couldn't swim, dive, or do anything at all. Like a man buried up to his neck in sand, he was held while the thunderous impact decimated the surf zone.

I was shocked at the ferocity, the gravity, the mercilessness. Where was he? Would he be drowned? Dismembered? It seemed entirely possible that his head could be torn clean off. When the set was finished with him, he popped up, shaken but alive. Any comfort we might have gained from his survival was swept away by the shock of the encounter. We knew he had been lucky.

A day of huge surf by modern standards is a cataclysmic event. An ocean swell of 20 feet can double in height on impact, then explode with enough energy to light a city or flatten a town. Ocean swells are unpredictable, dangerous, and occasionally grow to 50 feet and beyond. Until recently, only a few brave souls in Hawaii challenged huge swells. The Hawaii-centric view of the big-wave universe has crumbled over the past ten years, and a new frontier, previously known as the "Unridden Realm," has become a playground. The biggest wave, the thickest barrel, the worst wipeout—each bar rises as ensuing generations make their mark. Surfers off the coast of California are frolicking on massive peaks far beyond our

predecessors' wildest dreams. Suddenly, the small community of big-wave riding has grown, and the activity has aroused the world.

Jeff Clark first rode Maverick's in 1975. I was an awkward eight-year-old living in Connecticut, Peter Mel was just getting his water wings, and Jay Moriarity would not arrive for years. It would be 1990 before anyone took notice of Jeff's accomplishments, but he knew something special was rumbling beyond those jagged rocks near Half Moon Bay, and he wasn't going to wait. Those were quiet years for big-surf challenges. Small-wave performance was at center stage, and an adventurer like Mark Renneker could travel to Waimea Bay to find it desolate and perfect. Jeff's discovery would hang on the vine, ripening in obscurity.

Meanwhile, just a few miles down the coast, some of the world's best surfers were honing their craft in Santa Cruz and turning heads at places like Sunset Beach in Hawaii. Richard Schmidt led the charge, winning everyone's respect and admiration with his consistent performances in the islands. He earned an invitation to the 1990 Eddie Aikau contest at Waimea, and soon became California's leading authority on 20-foot surf. It would be Richard, with experience and credibility beyond reproach, whose historic session would finally break the Maverick's story to the surfing world.

Why are we fascinated by big waves? What compels someone to venture into the most treacherous conditions of the year, or the decade? Giant surf touches some of us at our core, delivering a primal jolt to our inner selves, and making us feel alive like few things in the modern world. When Captain Cooke came across the first wave-riding heathens in Hawaii, he noted the supreme pleasure the natives seemed to derive from the act. Centuries later, surfing transcends cultural boundaries, language barriers, and time itself. Is the magical force that compelled Cooke to wander the Pacific in ships (and the Polynesians in canoes) the same thing that lures us into the surf? Perhaps we are answering the proverbial call of the wild within us, and the attraction is innate.

I first witnessed this wonder of nature in full bloom on January 29, 1992, the day Schmidt charged a 50-foot Maverick's tube, and I have been mesmerized by it ever since. Though I barely got near the great waves that morning—in fact, they stunned and horrified me—I left the water giddy and eager for more. Maverick's has captivated me, just as I was charmed by the surf as a child in New Jersey. I am drawn to the hunt each season, and I find the pursuit more thrilling and rewarding than I had dared to imagine.

GRANT WASHBURN IN HIS
ELEMENT. FEBRUARY 1996.

RICHARD SCHMIDT, WITH HIS UNCANNY ABILITY TO MAKE
SENSE OF A BIG, GNARLY SWELL, DECEMBER 1992.

INTRODUCTION

RICHARD SCHMIDT

(Editor's note: Richard Schmidt caught a wave for the ages at the 1990 Eddie Aikau contest in Hawaii. Pulling off an electrifying air-drop and making it off the bottom, Schmidt scored a perfect 100, one of the most memorable rides in Waimea Bay's long history.)

When I dropped in on that wave at Waimea, I thought nothing could be as gnarly. I called my brother Dave, back in Santa Cruz, and was just frothing about it—the quality of the waves, the caliber of surfing, to this day one of the most incredible days of my life.

The next day, that same swell hit Maverick's. Dave was there with Tom Powers and Jeff Clark, the day that changed everything. When he called me that night, he was frothing worse than I was. He was just going off, like, "You would not believe this spot! You could fit semitrucks in these barrels! It's right there in Half Moon Bay!" Just on and on and on.

I couldn't believe what I was hearing. Here's my brother telling me to bring my Waimea board back home. Usually in California, a "gun" would be like 7'4" or 7'6". But I did bring my Hawaii gun, and that spring we had some great sessions at Maverick's.

I was shocked when I first paddled out there and saw 25-foot surf by anyone's measurement. The sheer volume of the waves reminded me of Hawaii, where I routinely spent three to six months a year surfing big waves. To think that there was a wave like this in California—it was just unbelievable. The place had the size and energy of Waimea, except that the Bay is much more inviting. You've got the warm blue water, the lifeguard on the beach, just a whole "come surf me" kind of thing. Maverick's was more foreboding and ominous, as challenging as any wave I'd surfed in my life. Probably more challenging, because when the wave hits the reef, it instantly jacks up five to eight feet and if you're not in the perfect spot, you're either going to get pitched or you won't be able to get over the ledge. And there's no comparison on the length of ride. The way Maverick's keeps jacking up, one bowl after another, makes it infinitely longer than any other big wave.

In those early days, going out with Jeff and Vince Collier and the crew, we knew that people were going to die out there. Especially the way people started charging it in the early '90s, almost oblivious to the consequences. It's not like Hawaii, where you might go from an 8'6" board to a 9'0" over two different swells. These California guys were going from a 7'6" to a 10'0", and that's a huge jump. People were just getting destroyed out there. But over the years, there's a crew that has mastered the spot. They've got their equipment tuned in and the right approach, and that's really nice to see. I think they're just now tapping into the potential of how to ride the spot.

Over the past few years, tow-ins have taken the spotlight on the biggest days, and I think that's a big part of the future for Maverick's. There's a lot of controversy on this issue, and I can definitely see both sides. On one hand, tow-in guys will never get the rush of harnessing a wave under their own power. They'll never get that feeling of doing it on their own, that tremendous sense of accomplishment. But then again, it's frustrating to know that it's almost impossible for a paddle-in surfer to get on or behind the peak of a big Maverick's wave. I think it's technically possible to paddle into a 30-footer, but so many variables have to come together, it's extremely difficult.

Myself, I'd rather ride a 30-foot wave on my tow board, just to place myself exactly where I want. When you see someone do that, all that speed and maneuverability on a small board, it's incredibly fun and exhilarating. I'll never forget watching that one big day (October '99) when Peter Mel, Kenny Collins, and Jeff Clark were the only ones out on one of the biggest swells they've ever had at Maverick's. I walked up to the cliff and just sat there, mesmerized by the waves they were getting towed into. There was one ridiculously giant wave where Peter kind of delayed his bottom turn and still made it—just insane. I knew right then that I had to get a little piece of this. As time goes on, I'd like to think we can work things out where Maverick's will be the ultimate paddle-in spot *and* a tow-in venue when it really gets big.

We're so fortunate as surfers, because we can enjoy our sport so much longer than a lot of athletes. As I get older, with a family and children, I'm starting to come to grips with what can happen out there. Years ago I was ready to go—any time, anywhere—if that was my day. And I still like to surf there once or twice a winter, when the conditions look right. But I've reached the point where I want to be around to see my kids grow up.

THE LOGISTICS

1. THE STANDARD PADDLE-OUT AREA. At high tide, in swells below 20 feet, this can be a smooth, twenty-five-minute trip through blue water. When giant swells combine with low tide and a relentless current, the channel fills with onrushing whitewater and the trip can take forty-five minutes or longer. Even the best Maverick's surfers have been known to turn back after an hour's struggle. As Kenny Collins described the worst-case scenario, "Constant fourth down and a hundred yards to go."

2. THE TRIP AROUND BLACKHAND REEF. This means a mile-long paddle, a real test of endurance, but on 20- to 25-foot swells, it's the path of least resistance. At 30 feet, everything changes. "Waves start breaking all the way across the bay," says Grant Washburn, "and I'm talking about 60-foot faces that look like Tahiti, just sucking dry. You can't be near that. On a huge day in 2004, I saw things out there I'd rather not see again."

3. THE SHORTCUT THROUGH THE LEFTS. Big-time gamble. Completely out of the question on big days. With a bit of luck, during long-period swells with the current running to the south, this can be done in fifteen minutes. "The worst of it can be at the very end," says Washburn. "You're through the shorebreak, you can see guys in the lineup *right* there, and you just want to cut straight across the pit. Really bad idea if a set's coming."

4. THE ROCKS. Caught inside with a south-to-north current at high tide, and no help from a Jet Ski, you *will* go through the rocks. Experienced Maverick's surfers recognize four passable gaps. Heading northward from Mushroom Rock, the holes get increasingly smaller (the fourth, alongside the biggest pile of rocks, is around five feet wide and the most difficult to negotiate). Knowledge and experience means a safe trip into the lagoon, and keeping a board is advisable for a belly ride at higher tides. Low tide doesn't mean an easy exit, just a better chance of walking the area once delivered through the rocks. Crucial: Have a leash that can be instantly unhooked. Once it gets tangled around a rock, you become its prisoner.

"I'll always always remember how heavy it looked the first time I paddled out. I went right over to the bowl, turned around, took off on the first wave and called Richie Schmidt off it [laughter]. He's paddling hard and I'm all, 'Hey-hey-hey!' and he backed out of it. I was stoked, but as soon as I got to the bottom and went through the foamball from the first wave, I started doing spinners and just ate it. Took two sets on the head, washed me all the way to the rocks, got held down, filled my wetsuit with water. I was like, 'OK, this place is heavy.'" — SHAWN RHODES

FIRST-TIME VIEW

MATT AMBROSE

(In the manner of many surfing legends, Matt Ambrose speaks through his actions. Just by nature, through experience and commitment, he tends to sit deepest in the pack. No surfer in Northern California is more respected, and the Maverick's contest has crystallized his reputation. Ambrose was a finalist in 2000, 2004, and 2006, and he won the coveted Jay Moriarity Award in the 2005 event.)

Where I come from, big-wave surfing is a local tradition. Dick Keating showed everyone the way, and as I got a little older, I started following Shawn Rhodes around. Whatever he surfed, I surfed. It's not that I set out to ride big waves. That was just the accepted way to go. Spots like Pumphouse, Pedro Point, and Sharp Park were the best Pacifica had to offer.

The first season I saw Maverick's, 1988–89, I just watched. I was right out of high school and I didn't feel I was ready for it—mostly because I thought it was a left! That's all we ever saw when we checked it out from the cliffs above the parking lot. I mean, a young regularfoot

MARK RENNEKER: "The first time I ever surfed the place, in 1990 with John Raymond, we figured out we should paddle out in the lagoon, but after it got dark, we got this brilliant idea to come in a different way—on the north side. Waves were exploding on the rocks, we were paddling back and forth trying to figure it out, and finally a huge surge of whitewater caught both of us. We were tumbled and thrashed, and both wound up on the dry-reef area, unhurt, boards akimbo. We thought it was the funniest thing ever. But we never did it again."

going out to surf a giant, hollow left? I was never interested.

Then one day I walked around the front with Jeff Clark and my friend Jim Kibblewhite, and it was like . . . oh, my God. Are you kidding? The right looked as perfect as Rincon. Jeff made us a bunch of boards that spring, and I remember going down to Santa Cruz to pick them up from Vince Collier, who was sanding them all. Flea [Virostko] and all the West Side guys were there, checking it out and figuring, "Whoa, these guys must be serious if they're getting *these* boards." I can still remember sitting in the van that day. I think we all realized the same thing. It was time to make a move.

When I first paddled out at Maverick's in the early '90s, I was way overconfident. I'd charged some pretty big waves around Northern California, and I'd been over to Kauai, and I thought we were gonna kill it on our 8'6"s and 9'0"s. Then I got out there, and I didn't even get a wave. The way the bottom drops out, the sheer height of the wave, the way those 30-foot faces just drain, like death waves—it was so much different than it looked from the cliff. It was no Rincon.

Rhodes didn't even have a board for that day. He was out on an 8'2" with Collier, Clark, Richard Schmidt, Kibblewhite, and myself. He took off on four waves, and on every one he either got launched or couldn't get enough speed off the bottom. But just to see him going off that hard was impressive. Collier and Clark were rushing it. Schmidt was getting bombs. I just wasn't ready to go in that bowl. And I couldn't believe how much bigger it was than the 8-to-10 foot day we left behind. It was like the swell had just come up after we paddled out.

I finally caught a wave my next time out there. The initial takeoff wasn't a big deal, but it turned into this glassy, crazy suck-out, and when I got to the bottom, I just stopped. I basically got run over, just totally mauled. Coming up, I'd been worked so hard my eyes couldn't focus at first, and I thought I'd blown out my eardrum. I kind of freaked out, but a little later that winter, I rode a really long

22

HAWAII'S PAUL MORENO NOT ONLY BROUGHT A
WORLDLY PERSPECTIVE TO MAVERICK'S, HE
SURFED IT AS WELL AS ANYONE. DECEMBER 1993.

TERRY AHUE, HAWAIIAN WATER PATROL: "I can't believe anyone goes into water this cold. I also can't believe guys surf in front of those frickin' rocks."

one that lasted close to a minute. That was it, I was sold. There was no going back.

In those early days, there was nobody around—maybe six to eight people who rode the place regularly—so you could try whatever you wanted, every session. You could learn to approach the bowl without going madman, because it wasn't crowded. I remember Paul Moreno came out once, and this is a guy who'd surfed big waves all over the world. He said, "Dude, if you grew up here, you don't have to go *anywhere*. Because this is the best big wave I've ever seen, period." We were all afraid to call it the size it really was, just because of politics and the whole Hawaii thing. We're calling it like 12 to 15 feet. And he goes, "Are you kidding? I just came from Waimea, where everybody was saying 20 feet, and this is just as big." That really justified things in our minds—not to mention that Moreno showed up on a single-fin board, ten feet long, barely three inches thick, and he went off harder than anyone had to that point. That basically sparked my interest in the single-fin thing. I own ten Thrusters, but what do you think you're gonna do at Maverick's, floaters? It's all about dropping down a huge face and making big, long turns. To this day, when Maverick's gets real, I'm on a single-fin out there.

It's funny. When we were growing up, Sharp Park was our big-wave spot. When Mav's came onto the scene, it just vanished. I don't think we ever paddled out there again.

25

STORMSURF

MARK SPONSLER

(Aside from being a regular in the Maverick's lineup, Mark Sponsler runs the www.stormsurf.com Web site, a veritable forecasting bible. If Sponsler says the swell will arrive around 2 P.M., you'll find more than a few surfers hitting the water at 1:30.)

To understand Maverick's, you need to understand waves. And to understand waves, you need to understand weather. Wind makes waves. Whether you're at Maverick's or Malibu, the physical process is the same. Large waves are created by strong wind blowing over the ocean in the same direction for a long time. The larger the area the wind blows over, the larger the waves become.

Florida hurricanes create a lot of wind. A Category 5 hurricane, the strongest of the lot, has sustained wind speeds reaching 155 mph or greater. Over time, these ragged, wind-driven waves start to radiate outward in all directions, escaping the direct influence of the storm's wrath. For a visual image, imagine dropping a pebble in a pond. But in a hurricane, the largest waves race ahead of the storm's direction of travel, and the choppy character of what is now a moving mountain of water starts to fade, revealing what is called a swell. The swells separate and become more uniformly spaced. If you were on a

GIANT, OUT-OF-CONTROL DAY WITH SETS BREAKING A QUARTER-MILE FROM THE NORMAL BREAK. JANUARY 2001.

DOUG ACTON: "Peter Mel on the October 28 swell in 1999, in my mind the biggest, most perfect day ever at Mav's. The Papa buoy's last reading, before the storm mowed it down, was 53 feet at 17 seconds. I expected a huge media circus, but Peter Mel and Skinny Collins were the only surfers in the water when the sun came up. They proceeded to tear the place apart, a tow-in show that didn't even seem real at the time. Jeff Clark eventually came out, and Flea tried to paddle into a few (to no avail) before towing, but this was the Peter Mel show. He was so ahead of the game, it was ridiculous. When we got back to the ramp, there was still nobody around. We were laughing like a bunch of kids in a candy store."

stationary boat several hundred miles ahead of the storm, you could measure the time of successive swells passing under you. A normal "period" between hurricane swells would be 11 to 14 seconds, with a height reaching maybe 10 to 12 feet.

By most standards, these would be considered big waves. You would not venture out in these conditions to swim, boat, or even surf unless you were highly capable or had a death wish. Waves of this magnitude can cause severe beach erosion, make channels impassable, and destroy oceanfront property. But hurricane swells pale in comparison to Northern California surf, because all 12-foot waves are not the same. Some will seem to move a lot more water and travel much faster. The period is what makes the difference. The longer the period, the faster and stronger the wave. Pure chop has a period of 4 to 8 seconds, windswell 9 to 11 seconds, weak swell 13 to 15 seconds and strong swell 16 seconds or greater. Though a hurricane can generate waves with periods in the 14-second range, storms headed for Maverick's can generate waves with periods at 25 seconds or greater, the most powerful waves on Earth short of a tidal wave.

Maverick's waves come from large winter storms that cross the deep waters of the North Pacific south of the Aleutian Islands. During the storm season, moist, energetic, and unstable tropical air streams form off the West Pacific coast of Japan, while cold, dry, and stable air pushes eastward over Siberia. The cold Siberian air eventually reaches the open waters of the Pacific between the Kuril Islands and Kamchatka Peninsula, where a grand collision occurs. The two different air masses do not combine. Like a bulldozer clearing a path through a forest, the eastward-moving air mass plows the warmer air up in front of it. A building volume of moist air starts rising in front of the bulldozer's blade, causing surface pressure to drop at the boundary between the two air masses. The more warm air that gets displaced upward, the deeper the pressure falls. High in the atmosphere, the storm taps the jet stream to evacuate the rising air, further escalating the pressure difference down at the surface.

The building tower of moist air starts spinning counterclockwise. Nature desperately tries to establish some sort of equilibrium at the ocean's surface, and the cold Siberian air starts rushing eastward to fill the hole. This only serves to drive more warm air upward, intensifying the storm. It is this rapid movement of cold air from the west to the east that creates wind. The greater the pressure difference, the greater the wind.

What puts Maverick's in a league of its own is its location. When a storm pushes east off the Kuril Islands, it has only 1,900 nautical miles of open ocean to cover before it hits the Hawaiian Islands. This gives the storm a rather limited space in which to grow, mature, and generate waves. Conversely, Maverick's is positioned on the far eastern side of the Pacific, giving the storm all 3,300 nautical miles of the North Pacific Ocean in which to mature. Even storms that develop east of the dateline have ample room to grow before impacting the Canadian coast. Maverick's is 850 miles farther north than Hawaii, positioning it to receive swells head-on rather than at an oblique angle.

While Maverick's tends to receive better, more direct swells than Hawaii, local winds play a huge factor. Even the smallest amount of chop on the wave's face can send a surfer out of control. Offshore winds, normally the most favorable for small-wave riding (and generally preferred in Hawaiian big surf), make for harrowing conditions at Maverick's. These winds accelerate as they move up the huge face of a Maverick's wave, making it nearly impossible for a rider to drop in. Surfers typically get hung up at the top of the wave or blown off the back altogether. Even if you succeed in dropping in, the likelihood of getting airborne and not connecting at the bottom is high. Jay Moriarity's infamous cover-shot wipeout from December 1994 is a prime example.

If Maverick's were a few hundred miles farther north, the jet stream would drive storm energy over it and create bad local wind conditions. If Maverick's were a few hundred miles to the south, it would not receive as much direct swell energy, and the waves would be smaller. As it is, it's located in an ideal position to receive an amazingly consistent supply of big waves. During the winter of 1998–99, a relatively unimpressive year meteorologically, Grant Washburn, Mark Renneker, and John Raymond had a friendly competition to see who could ride Maverick's most often. La Niña was in control of the weather pattern, and while huge storms were not the norm, there was an abundant supply of smaller localized storms. When the season was over, they had surfed the place over eighty separate days, an unheard-of quantity for any big-wave break (by comparison, a good winter at Peahi would yield perhaps thirty rideable days).

The Maverick's crew is well versed in the art of surf forecasting—and they need to be. A change in the weather can mean the difference between life and death out there. Checking the forecast charts, wave models, and buoys online is as much a part of the daily routine as checking the surf with your naked eyes. Maverick's is at its prime

from late October through March, and a good season can last much longer. During the epic El Niño winter of 1997–98, the first ever to be successfully forecast, Maverick's awoke on September 15 with 30-foot sets and a remarkable 25-second period. Wavelengths of this magnitude are normally reserved for the dead of winter, but this one hit during the summer—and it was just the beginning. More large swells followed, building in intensity and frequency. On January 25, 1998, a huge storm developed off the Siberian coast, the twenty-fourth significant-class one of the season. It tracked due east for three days with winds blowing at 50 to 65 knots for 48 hours. Seas of nearly 50 feet were reported covering a large area aimed directly at Maverick's and in a lesser degree toward Hawaii. On January 28, the huge swell hit Oahu's North Shore, where Ken Bradshaw towed into the biggest wave ever ridden.

Two days later, the same swell hit Maverick's. Outer buoys indicated seas at 30.8 feet at 20 seconds, and the Half Moon Bay buoy showed 20 at 20. A few brave souls succeeded in paddling out to Maverick's, but most were sent back to the beach unrewarded. It was really too big for effective paddle-surfing, and the tow-in movement hadn't really caught on in Northern California. One tow team did make it out and successfully rode wave faces in the 50-foot-plus range. If anything, it was a wake-up call for what was to follow. More swells continued as the season marched on, and 20-to-25-foot swells (40-foot faces) became so consistent, by the latter part of the season it was getting hard to find people to surf with. Everyone was burned out. It finally shut down in mid-June of '98, nine months after it began. During that season we counted thirty-six major storms, with many smaller ones left off the books.

With the growth of tow surfing, the push to ride bigger waves opened up a whole new horizon at Maverick's. Waves that were previously considered untouchable by paddle-in surfers are now ridden with relative ease. On October 27, 1999, during the peak of La Niña, the tow teams got their first real opportunity to tap the full potential of Maverick's when the first significant-class storm of the season developed 950 nautical miles off the Oregon coast. Though forecast to be only moderately strong by the models, pressure unexpectedly dropped and the winds reached 65 knots. It held for 24 hours, all aimed right at Northern California and Maverick's.

The center of the fetch area moved directly over outer buoy 46006, where winds were clocked at 48 knots gusting to 68. This generated seas ranging from 51 feet at 20 seconds to 53.4 feet at 17 seconds.

DOUG ACTON: "Noah Johnson took a wipeout in the 2000 contest that would have sent a normal surfer packing and never looking back. Noah returned with a vengeance the following winter and caught this bomb on one of the few swells ever to break on the third reef. Standing on my waverunner, camera in my left hand, throttle in the other, I raced to the top of the massive wave in front. As soon as I had a clear view of the beast, I let go of the gas and started firing. It's one of the biggest waves ever ridden at Mav's."

The swell slammed into Maverick's the next day. By sunrise, the Half Moon Bay buoy jumped to the red line with seas at 18 feet at 20 seconds, eventually reaching 20 at 17. Because the storm was relatively near shore, the shorter-period chop component didn't have time to decay as the swell radiated away from the fetch area. A high tide allowed all the swell's raw and unrefined energy to move through the distant reefs unfettered, focusing even more intensely on Maverick's. Paddle-in surfing was out of the question, but a few tow teams were in heaven. Peter Mel and Skindog Collins scored the biggest waves ever at Maverick's, estimated at nearly 70 feet on the face.

The following year, on December 19, 2000, the ninth storm of the season formed, north of Hawaii and west of Washington. Some 36 hours later, the pressure had dropped to 970 mbs with winds at 50 to 65 knots. Seas built to 42 feet and held. Again, the outer buoy jumped to an unbelievable 48.2 feet at 17 seconds, but without the raging winds reported during the previous year's big storm. The next morning, three days before Christmas, the swell hit Maverick's. The Half Moon Bay buoy maxed out with seas reaching 22 feet at 17 seconds. And again, the tow teams were primed and in position. But instead of Pete, Skinny, and Jeff Clark having the break all to themselves, an international flotilla had converged to ride wave faces near 70 feet.

Conversely, several weeks later, another strong storm formed in much the same location of the northeast Pacific. But the high-pressure dome that had tenuously protected Maverick's had broken down. The storm front moved through unabated, making local conditions miserable. Squall lines were racing eastward, bringing rain and hard west winds. An ugly residual southwest windswell intermixed with a huge northwest ground swell, sending nasty warbles across the faces of what could have been another epic swell. It was pure storm surf. Some potential takers watched from the cliff, then headed home in search of warmth, but a few of us walked out to the point for a closer inspection. Climbing fifty feet up the cliff, we watched as set after set unloaded on the reef, peeling perfectly except for the cross-chop that littered the lineup. Out toward the horizon, a large cabin cruiser muscled its way northward, presumably racing toward the safety of the San Francisco Bay. We were stunned to watch it completely disappearing in the troughs between giant waves. Not even the antenna on the top of the bridge was visible. We agreed the swells were 40 feet and the breaking waves were 60 feet—probably much more.

At that moment, we were struck by the realization that even with all the hype and media attention Maverick's has received, its real big-wave potential hasn't even been scratched. Unfathomable as that may seem, all the evidence points that way. The reef has never had a problem holding anything the North Pacific has thrown at it. You never hear that Maverick's is unrideable due to size or form, only because of equipment limitations. With that no longer a factor, thanks to the new standard of Jet Skis and tow boards, it's time to move forward. From a historical perspective, the giant swells of 1999 and 2000 were just the first steps on the journey—and meteorologically, those storms were wimps. Strong La Niña conditions dominated the global weather pattern. Storms were episodic, short-lived, and local. High pressure controlled the East Pacific, driving the larger systems northward into the Aleutians, disrupting their fetch pattern. The average significant fetch time per storm was below normal, as were sea heights. The big tow-swells of 1999 and 2000 were short-lived, small in areal coverage, and not particularly deep. Their one redeeming factor was they were local, so every bit of swell energy arrived unimpeded. But in reality they were anomalies, like a big fish in a small bowl, the high points in otherwise lackluster years.

It's time to race toward the 100-foot watermark. The Big One would occur most likely in January, forming off Siberia and barreling through the North Pacific corridor untouched by high pressure. It would be the proverbial bull in a china shop, creating days of driving fetch and mountainous seas before tracking northward, some 900 miles northwest of Pillar Point, by localized high pressure. The high would check the storm's cold front just before it reached the coast, defusing the winds, smoothing the ocean surface and providing a clean slate for the monster. Near-shore buoy readings of 25 feet at 25 seconds would result in 80-to-90-foot faces. With the recent passing of La Niña, the door is open once again to El Niño. Its influence enhances the North Pacific winter storm track and adds fuel to developing systems, setting up potentially ideal conditions. We're positioned to explore a whole new world of big-wave surfing at Maverick's. It's a waiting game now.

SURF FORECASTER MARK SPONSLER IS A MAVERICK'S REGULAR ON BIG DAYS.

PEOPLE WONDER WHY SURFERS DON'T TAKE OFF ON THE PEAK. SHANE DESMOND NEGOTIATES THE MAELSTROM.

SHAWN RHODES: "I never go online or follow the charts. I figure I'm right here, and if it's big, the only thing that can screw it up is the wind—and having a second kid [laughter]. I just wake up, look at the little flag I've got on my roof, and it's on."

GRANT WASHBURN: "When it's blowing hard offshore, that's a dream situation at most spots. At Maverick's it's a nightmare. You get held back, caught up in the lip. Maybe it doesn't break at all, or maybe it breaks so fiercely you just fly through the air. I mean, being caught up high on a 35-foot face, then blown out the front, you're in a world you never imagined when you looked at the pictures."

35

> "We're all pretty good friends out there. We pass the time, talk story, board design, whatever comes up. But on the big days, when the real sessions happen, not a word is spoken. Literally. I've been out on days when not a word was said between us. You've got to focus all your energy on being in the right place." — PETER MEL

THE LINEUP

JOHN RAYMOND

(John Raymond lives for Maverick's. It often seems he lives AT Maverick's. While most surfers pick their spots, weighing every issue from fear to magazine exposure, Raymond keeps it simple. He's there for every swell. Out of Pacifica, and known for his feats of endurance at huge Ocean Beach, Raymond makes up for his performance limitations with pure stoke and desire.)

Surfers generally don't show much respect for each other, and it turns a lot of people off to the sport. You know, stay off my wave, don't come to our spot, don't even pull in to the parking lot. What attracts me to Maverick's is that it's *nothing* like that. People out there respect each other, stick up for each other. There's a real brotherhood in the water, because you're going through something so heavy, everybody feels they're in it together. It might be the main reason I surf there as often as I do.

On the other hand, you can be having a good ol' time out there, making all your waves, yukking it up with your friends, and then something goes wrong. You're out of position, you get caught inside or fall off a wave, and all of a sudden you're facing your maker. You're doing everything possible just to stay alive. And that's another

unusual thing about Maverick's: In a situation like that, no matter how many people might be out there, nobody can help you.

As a result, you don't hear guys being too cocky out there. It's cool to talk about your waves, share that with your friends, but not to feel like you're "the man" or just owning it. Because the next one could kill you. It's a totally different feeling than sticking one at Steamer Lane or your favorite point break. It's more like you're in awe of what happened, and you're grateful for it.

For years, I'd go out and know every single person in the lineup. That's not always the case now, and we're getting a few more loose cannons—people who don't realize that they'll be in the pit eventually, and there will be ten more waves coming, and they'll really see that they could die. All of a sudden they turn all white, they're throwing up, maybe bleeding from a couple of places, and that shuts them up for good.

I think part of survival out there is being able to loosen up. Jay Moriarity was the all-time classic. You could be in the middle of a conversation with him, and then he'd stroke into a wave, and he'd keep talking right through the drop, just laughing his head off. There wasn't one cocky thing about it. That's pure enjoyment of the experience. Take just one trip to a crowded small-wave spot, where everybody's pissed off and snapping at each other, and you see the difference.

I'd like to think we have an atmosphere like surfers had in the early 1950s, when there was real camaraderie in the water, guys brought together by the big-wave experience. That's the beauty of Maverick's; it's something we all have in common. If I see another Mav's surfer in a bar, it's like he's a brother to me. We've surfed the place together. The best example is Doc [Renneker] and Flea. You could travel the world and not find two personalities so different. But Maverick's makes them veritable friends, and they totally respect each other. A big, dangerous wave has brought them together.

There was a guy who used to surf Maverick's who was a little loose in the head. We didn't have any sort of connection with each other at all. But one time, we were the only two guys in the water and I got unbelievably thrashed. I missed a wave, took a horrendous set in the face, got washed into Sail Rock, bounced off the reef and stuff, and it was bad. Really shook me up. I was sort of staggering around the reef on the north side, and this guy went looking for me. Comes running up, hugging me and stuff, I couldn't believe it. But it was cool. That's the kind of thing that happens here.

Surfers earn two kinds of respect: for skill, and for courage. But there's a fine line between courage and stupidity. Some guys do a lot of crazy things, but you don't respect them because their courage seems almost fake, like they're doing it just to get photographed. Kodak courage, we call it. All kinds of surfers pull that stuff on a bright, clear morning. Guys with true courage, like Jay, stick it on a dark, foggy afternoon with nobody there. If somebody you've never seen comes paddling out and immediately sits right next to Matt Ambrose, he's either stupid or he's cocky and not respectful. We don't get the kind of thing you see in Hawaii, where guys are physically chased out of the water, but somebody like Grant or Jeff Clark will sound them out. Like, "You're a danger to yourself and everybody out here. You should get off the peak and think about things a while." There's no need to get *too* angry. It's like Grant says: Nobody's gonna tell you to get lost, because if you're not good enough to take that drop, you *are* lost.

It's always interesting to check out some of the personalities in such a heavy environment. Like Skindog [Collins], he first struck me as a cocky little kid; I figured there's no way I'd ever like him. But he's not like that at all. He's a really open, nice guy, and as good as he is, he's really respectful of people. I really think Maverick's has brought out the best in him. Doc is the best guy you could possibly have out there with you. Most people, in heavy situations, they only want to talk about their rides. Doc wants to talk about *your* wave. That's part of the brotherhood. I'm the same way; if Grant gets a great wave, half the time I enjoy it more than he did.

Vince Collier is the guy who introduced most of the Santa Cruz guys to Maverick's, and he tends to play the sheriff wherever he goes. You know—"I'm gonna kick your ass!" and that sort of thing. I've seen those guys show up at 5:30 in the morning with Vince leading the way, got the cigarettes, playing heavy metal as loud as it can get, and they're just *screaming.* "Yeah! Fuckin' right on!" God, those guys get amped.

But I remember this one huge day, I was paddling up the face of a wave, just barely making it, and when I turned and looked down, there was Vince, just stuck like a dog in the pit. All I saw was his face, mouth wide open, and this look of sheer terror in his eyes. Here's this big, intimidating guy, but Maverick's put the fear in him.

Ken Bradshaw, who shaped a lot of my boards in the early years, was always very defensive of his home breaks in Hawaii. He didn't think anything here could compare. But he was awestruck by Maverick's. You could see that instantly. I remember Grant, Ambrose,

LINEUP AT THE CEREMONY CHRISTENING THE 2000 CONTEST. FAR LEFT: SARAH AND MIKE GERHARDT.

GATHERING AT THE CAFE AFTER THE GIANT SURF OF OCTOBER 28, 1999. CLOCKWISE FROM BOTTOM CENTER: JAY MORIARITY, JEFF CLARK, JEFF HARRISON, NEIL MATTHIES, MIKE BRUMETT, GRANT WASHBURN, KENNY COLLINS AND WIFE ANNOUSCHKA, WILL SMITH.

KENNY COLLINS: "On a big day, you're not really out there chattin'. It's not like First Peak at the Lane, hanging out with your friends. You might hear some outsider dealin' with his demons, though. Psyching himself up, trying to justify something, thinking about not gettin' murdered . . . weird stuff."

JOSH LOYA: "The worst kind of a guy is a small-wave surfer who has decided to make his mark. He's cluttering up the lineup, just to say he was there. 'Yeah, I was charging, man. Pete Mel was out, Flea, all the heavy guys, and I got like two good waves.' Yeah, two small ones on the shoulder. Then the idiot's friends want to come out and do it."

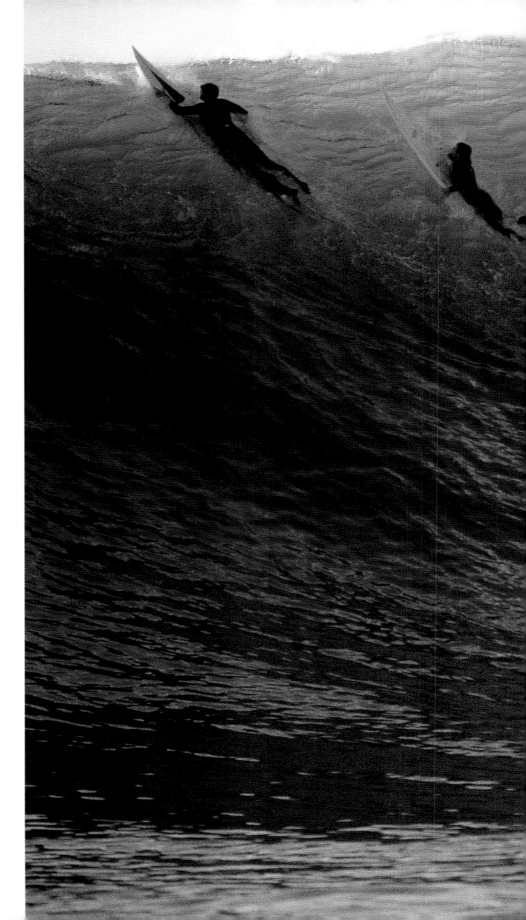

GRANT WASHBURN: "You hear guys laughing, but sometimes it's nervous laughter. It's sort of like a horror movie, where you're on the edge of your seat and so scared, you'll laugh at anything. Out at Maverick's, the jokes are funnier."

and I were out with Kenny on a really big day. Grant took off on a bomb, and I turned to Bradshaw and said, "Wow, that wave was 20 foot." And he said, "More like 25." That's when I realized it's a real wave. Not that we ever thought it wasn't, but this was confirmation from a legend, and he wanted to know everything about it.

Brazilian surfers have sort of a sketchy reputation around the world, and I don't think that's fair, because it's ridiculous to throw out that kind of stereotype. But I've heard from the grapevine that with most of those guys, if you went to their local spot back home, they'd hassle you like crazy. If you surfed Trestles with them, you probably wouldn't have any fun. But out at Maverick's, they're just as friendly as they could be. They know that the consequence out-weighs the petty stuff. In fact, one of the scariest things I've ever experienced at Maverick's came in '98, when a relatively inexperi-enced Brazilian guy hit the water. It was one of the heaviest days we've ever had; the day Neil Matthies had that tombstoning, two-wave hold-down and nearly drowned. But this Brazilian guy got sucked over the falls, blew out his eardrum and really took a beat-ing. We heard this wailing moan . . . *Hellllp* . . . it was really eerie, sounded like he was dying. Everybody got silent after that, and if someone hadn't driven a boat in there to throw him a life preserver, he might not have made it.

No matter who you are, if you've never surfed Maverick's, you should sit way out in the channel for a while—for weeks, if that's what it takes. That's a smart surfer; that's what we want to see. Randy Cone [from San Francisco], time after time, did nothing but watch from the bluff. He was just hanging around; nobody could fig-ure out his story. Turns out he's one of the most talented surfers we've ever seen. He's exactly the example of what you should do. Here's the opposite of that: One of the first times he'd ever surfed the place, this guy paddles straight past everyone in the hierarchy, with Ambrose at the pinnacle, and sits deeper than everyone. We're all, "Who the hell is *this*?" It was a heavy, walled-up day out of the west, maybe ten waves in a set, and you didn't want to get caught inside for any reason. Well, this guy took off on one of the first waves of a set, way too deep, and just got buried. Ambrose said it was a horrible,

PADDLER'S VIEW FROM THE LEFT CHANNEL.
NOTE BELOW-SEA-LEVEL TROUGH.

horrible hold-down, with about eight more waves about to land on him. About an hour later, a helicopter landed on the reef, right behind Sail Rock. I knew it was this guy. I figured he was dead. Apparently he'd been hit by the fin of his board, slashed a huge cut in his leg, and he'd pretty much given up. He was lifeless, letting himself get pounded on the rocks. Just by luck, it was a really low tide, so people could go in there and save him. But with respect shown for the break, that doesn't happen.

Jeff Clark gets the most respect of all the surfers out there, and not just because he discovered the spot. He earns it every time he paddles out. When he turns for a wave, you don't even *think* about going. On the other hand, he tends to be up and down, emotionally. He can have his moods, fighting some cosmic debris, and I guess there are people who feel he's taken financial advantage of the spot. But for the most part, he's pretty serene. If he doesn't like what's going on, he gets real quiet and just leaves.

Talk about surfing when the cameras aren't around—there's one wave Jeff got I'll never forget, and it said everything about what he's like out there. This was about seven or eight years ago, a totally bleak, foggy afternoon. Maybe four of us were out, sitting right next to each other, when this absolute bomb of a wave came: 30 feet, solid, as heavy as Maverick's can produce. I paddled south for all I was worth, because I was scared to death. Jeff paddled out, and *at* the wave. Then he turned and went. No boats, no photographers, no reason for him to go. He made that wave, and when he came back out, there was a big smile on his face. I said, "Man, that was heavy." And he said, "Yeah, that was fun." That's Jeff. When he's sixty-five years old, if he turns to go, it's his wave, no matter who else is out there. He's the purest of the pure.

FOR 15 YEARS, THIS WAS THE LINEUP: JEFF CLARK, DEALING ONLY WITH HIS OWN DESIRE.

VINCE COLLIER TRIGGERED THE MIGRATION OF SANTA CRUZ SURFERS TO MAVERICK'S, RAISING THE STAKES AND THE TALENT LEVEL. DECEMBER 1993.

STEVE DWYER, MATT AMBROSE, JAY MORIARITY, AND KENNY COLLINS PADDLING OUT FOR A HEAT IN THE 2000 CONTEST. SETS RAN TO 25 FEET THAT DAY; REMOVE THE JERSEYS AND THE FACES WOULD BE THE SAME.

"Every year you sit around all summer and talk about how hard you're gonna charge the place, and then you get out there, and you don't get a whole lot of them. And when you do, there's never an easy one. It's a terrifying, vertical drop, and a 20-footer out there is like no other spot that we know about." — **MATT AMBROSE**

44

THE DROP

SHAWN RHODES

(Shawn Rhodes, owner of the NorCal surf shop in Pacifica, rode big waves in obscurity for years. He liked it that way. A disciple of Dick Keating and partner of Matt Ambrose, Rhodes was far more interested in big, nasty waves than any publicity he might get. The Maverick's contest brought him some long-overdue recognition, and there is justice in that. Every big-wave surfer should know his name.)

There's nothing like the drop at Maverick's. I can't think of anything that would compare to it. Maybe dropping off a cornice in the mountains, but even that's not the same, because you're strapped into your ski boots, and you didn't have to paddle into it.

It's the ultimate feeling, almost like being a bird—weightless, suspended, time slowing down all around you. On a really big one, you feel like you're dropping forever. And you never really get there, because you're always pulling a turn, trying to get to that next section, before you could ever fade to the bottom. That's what separates Maverick's from so many other spots: the constant jacking and doubling-up of the wave. There are times when the inside section is so heavy, you take a more critical drop in there than you did at the outset.

A MEETING OF NATURAL FORCES: THE MAVERICK'S DROP
AND HAWAIIAN GREAT BROCK LITTLE, 2000 CONTEST.

PERENNIAL CHARGER SHAWN RHODES,
TESTING HIS GUN TO THE LIMIT.

I don't think it's hard to catch a bomb out there if you really want it. You could take off underneath the pit on a 6'3" if you were that committed. The hard part is putting yourself in the right position: learning the wave, where the boil is, where the peak's going to be. Even today, after surfing the place more than ten years, I haven't quite figured out exactly my kind of wave at that place. But I'm not the guy who sits way outside. I like to be on the move, back and forth, to be in the pack but get waves from a different angle. Back in the day, I might have launched myself into anything. Now I'm looking for something I can make.

What can go wrong on the drop? A lot of things. Digging an edge right off the bat. Not quite figuring out that second ledge—and there's always a second ledge, especially at medium to low tide. Turning around like you're going to go, then maybe thinking it's not the right one, or someone else is going, and being too late—over the falls. Or the classic one of standing up before you actually have the wave and being hung out to dry, just launched over the lip.

I'm really careful about my boards, because I don't have a huge quiver of guns. I probably have the least amount of boards of all my friends—and I *shape* boards. So you learn not to make certain mistakes. There's a point where you have to go, no matter what, and that's something I just couldn't tell myself at Maverick's for the first four or five years I surfed it. You can pump yourself up for days about going out there and charging it, but when it actually comes time to throwing yourself over that ledge, you can't even have the slightest hesitation about it.

A couple of years ago, I was having a great session out there, ready to take the next one in. One of the Brazilian guys turned around late and took off, so I pulled back at the last second, didn't realize how late I was, and the lip hit the top of my board. Just a horrible wipeout. Broke my favorite board, almost brand new, a board that worked insane. There are other times where you bail out, then watch the wave back off a little and realize you should have gone. So now, I'm just going. No hesitation.

I've never been a shoulder-hopper, and I'm completely over the guys who pull that shit out there. It drives me nuts when I see it, because they don't even care. We're out there taking the biggest risks,

47

GRANT WASHBURN: "You have to outrun the beast. You have to want to make that drop so bad, you commit entirely. If you halfway don't want it, you won't come close."

48

EVAN SLATER, HANGING BY A THREAD. SOMETIMES,
EVEN ABSOLUTE COMMITMENT ISN'T ENOUGH.

2006 CONTEST WINNER GRANT (TWIGGY) BAKER
DEMONSTRATING PERFECT VERTICAL TRIM.

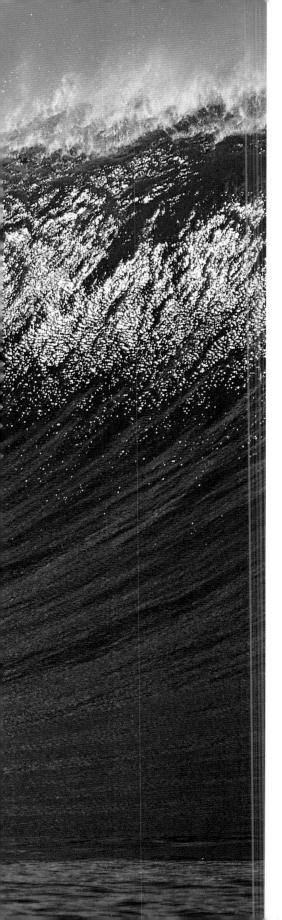

PETER MEL: "It's hard to explain, but the way I like to do it, I feel like I'm never really dropping. It's not like a roller-coaster to me, or an elevator. When I'm paddling into a wave, I never want to see a drop. I want to be *down* it. I don't want to move, I don't want to rise up. I want the wave to grow behind me. So as the wave is rising, and I'm dropping, it's like being suspended in space. That's why you seldom see me do one of those dramatic air-drops, like Flea or Evan Slater. When I'm doing things right, I'm suspended in space in my mind. You're really letting the wave do all the work. Then you punch the bottom and do the gravity thing."

going deep in the bowl, and these guys are fading us? I'm just super bitter about that. I can't say how many sessions I've had where I passed up five, ten waves where I could easily have dropped in on someone—just because I'm not going to be that person. I'm not gonna screw up the whole vibe. I mean, you're deep, you get to the bottom of the wave, and here's this guy in front of you, kind of off balance, or he's cranking off some dramatic turn like he's riding the wave of his life, and it's like, wait a minute. There's something wrong here.

The drop is heaviest out there at a super low tide. I went there on a minus tide one day with Matt Ambrose, Brent Heckerman, and my friend Ricky, who doesn't surf much anymore. We walked all the way to Mushroom Rock, timed the sets and jumped off there—that's how low it was. It was maybe a 12-to-15-foot swell, sheet glass, but these waves would come in and jack up another 6 to 8 feet, just *throwing*. On one takeoff I had a guy rush me from the shoulder, and I kind of hesitated, and it was probably the only wave to this day where I got to the bottom and pearled. As I was flying off, I looked up and the whole thing was tubing over me, just this giant cavern. I'll always have that picture in my mind: biggest tube I'd ever seen, looking up and catching a glimpse of Ricky's eyes, just trippin' as he sat up on the shoulder. And I just got murdered. My wetsuit ripped off, down to my waist, out to my arms, just done, and I got washed all the way through the rocks. But I paddled back out and had a great session after that.

On days like that, the place is fuckin' *heavy*. I don't care what anyone says about Jaws, Teahupoo, or wherever they're from, I guarantee you when it comes down to it, Maverick's is heavier. When NorCal guys go to Indo, we tend to do pretty well. No more 48-degree water, no more wetsuits, you've shed everything and you *really* feel good. I'll take off on anything down there. Just pull in, get barreled, no sponsors on my board, just riding for myself. But that's how it is when you go anywhere after Maverick's. At Teahupoo, the barrel's gnarly and the consequences deadly, but with the tropical water you're twice as loose and you feel twice as good. I like it shallow. I'd like to surf Teahupoo. They don't seem too interested in surfing here.

"I had a wipeout, years ago, that drove me all the way to the bottom. I was bouncing along the reef, then went deeper still into some chasm. I was thinking, 'This is really bad. I'm deeper than anyone's ever been out here.' I knew that if a second wave went over me, I was done. I was able to stay calm, knowing I'd practiced holding my breath for situations like this. But I've marked in my mind where it happened. I'm afraid of that place." — MARK RENNEKER

ANATOMY OF A WIPEOUT

EVAN SLATER

(Evan Slater was the first out-of-town "name" surfer to consistently ride Maverick's. For a number of locals, his presence legitimized the spot's growing appeal. Now the editor of Surfing *magazine, Slater has been a fearless, accomplished surfer at big-wave spots around the world. Known for his brazen dismissal of the consequences, he has also taken some of the most ferocious wipeouts ever witnessed.)*

Back in the early '90s, when Maverick's was just a cold, dark legend for most of us, I remember thumbing through some of the early articles on the spot and being completely in awe. Of course, the shots of guys like Richard Schmidt streaking off the bottom were impressive, but I was more blown away by the wipeouts. Tons of 'em. In all different moods, shapes, and sizes. Rod Walsha swan-diving from behind the bowl. Darin Bingham skipping out and bodysurfing a clean 18-footer. Rick "Frosty" Hesson lifted up and away in stiff, scary-looking offshores. They all looked like *Faces of Death* clips to me, but somehow these surfers seemed to bounce right back. As it said in a

MIKE BRUMETT'S EPIC FREEFALL DURING THE
2005 CONTEST. STYLE POINTS STILL IN PLAY.

EVAN SLATER, ENDURING PHASE 3
OF A CLASSIC MAVERICK'S TUMBLE.

Surfer's Journal caption on Walsha's horrific fall: "Badly shaken, he paddled back out to make the biggest wave of the day."

Huh? After the weight of the world just pile-drove him into fifteen feet of icy blackness, swirling and spinning and cartwheeling for what must have felt like an eternity? It didn't make sense to me. It also didn't make me too anxious to test it out myself. I mean, to survive wipeouts like that, those NorCal guys must be running the entire length of the San Francisco Bay. Underwater.

It wasn't long before I finally made it up there and surveyed the madness firsthand. As I found out during my virgin session on April 1, 1994, wipeouts are inevitable at Maverick's. No matter how good you are or what kind of equipment you're riding, if you challenge the bowl, you will lose a few battles. And when you do, it's a beating like no other paddle-in big wave in the world.

In order to understand this, you have to understand the wave itself. The takeoff zone in the bowl is only fifteen or twenty feet wide, covering both the left and the right. Swells march in as big, fat lumps, then double in size and fold over themselves as they hit the shelf. Within this zone, each wave has about a three-to-five-foot wide "ramp," or makeable entry point, with a one-to-two-second window of opportunity. The location of the ramp changes with every wave; sometimes it's not there at all. Mistime it by a split second or take off a foot too deep, and you'll be freefalling. Guaranteed. Even after surviving countless beatings and a handful of two-wave hold-downs, I still have no clue why there's a 99.9 percent wipeout survival rate at Maverick's. Every time you go through one, you wonder in midthrashing, "Is this the end for me?"

Since I've lived to tell about each and every one of them, I'm very familiar with the many stages of a Maverick's wipeout. Given that the most common ones find the bottom dropping out from under you on takeoff, I'll walk you through one of those:

1. The window of opportunity on the peak is so narrow that any charger will, from time to time, choose the wrong wave. With crowds and adrenaline at maximum capacity, sometimes you just have to go and hope for the best. As I'm paddling, I *must* have that "I'm making it at all costs" mentality. Even if my chances are slim, even a hint of hesitation or second-guessing could spell disaster. So I'm paddling under this ledge with my head down and eyes focused on making it to the bottom. The problem is, all the forces of nature are against me. The water rushing up the face carries the speed of a Class Five rapid, any hint of offshore wind will lift my board up and off the face, and that peak, which was just a big lump a second ago, is now

55

ROSS CLARKE-JONES: "For years, looking at photos, I couldn't understand why nobody sat on the peak. Now I get it. I'm not going in there."

56

PADDLING IN BEHIND THE PEAK, PETER MEL DIDN'T
DO ANYTHING WRONG—ASIDE FROM ATTEMPTING
THE IMPOSSIBLE. DECEMBER 11, 2000.

JOHN RAYMOND: "I don't know too many guys who have actually hit bottom out there. It happened to me on a day that wasn't that big. It was sort of a routine wipeout, but then about the biggest wave in three hours just sucked dry right in front of me. It was the most violent working I've ever had. I hit the bottom and bounced around there a couple more times, and after a few seconds, I got sucked right back down. My board just took a savage beating. Had a ding about every three inches. As Doc said, it looked like the barbarians came along with their rocks and slings."

a towering, four-story building. With nothing but hope to keep me glued to the face, there's no other alternative: I'm launching.

2. The first thing that comes to mind when I detach is, "Oh shit, I gotta stick this." Most of the time, it's wishful thinking. Too much speed, too much face, and those big, narrow guns aren't the most stable landing pads. So I try to stay over my board, spread out my arms like wings and prepare for touchdown.

3. Slap! Freefalls tend to make your board drift sideways, out toward the channel, and you'll land midface, completely off balance. I fall to the side, slap the water, and feel a sharp sting on my face and side as I try to penetrate. Usually, pulling out through the back just isn't in the cards. So, I try to ball up and prepare for the next phase.

4. The trip back over the falls is the most gloriously terrifying experience I know. On one hand, you've completely handed over all control to this big, cold beast of a wave. Whether she spits you out right away or chews on you for a while is entirely up to her. As I'm getting sucked back up the face and thrown out into space with the lip, I make sure to catch a quick peek. Suspended thirty feet above the flats and crunched in a little ball, I can see everything: the people lining the cliff, the Air Force facility, and those massive inside rocks I'm about to meet real soon. Under any other circumstance, I'd be moved by the view.

5. The landing is when you're at the greatest risk of injuring a body part. This is when the weight of the peak unloads on you, and if your leg or shoulder or knee is set up for it, Mav's will inflict damage. I stay in that ball position through this phase, transporting myself to some Black Flag mosh pit from my teen years and hoping no one sucker punches me.

6. Now it's time for my lungs to be tested. Going back up and over the falls is especially heavy at Mav's because there are so many deep, dark holes in the reef. The crashing lip sends white water spirals down to all of them, and more often than not, you get stuck in

EVEN THE BEST NORTHERN CALIFORNIA SURFERS GO DOWN. STEVE DWYER, FAR FROM PENETRATION.

DOUG ACTON: "In the early years, I did a lot of work from the tip of Pillar Point with my 800 lens. This was 1992, one of those golden days when the waves and light were perfect. Darin Bingham, who had been surfing well all winter, had to bail out at the top of this wave and actually bodysurfed down the face in perfect style. The drag of his leash eventually got him, but as far as I know, this is the biggest wave ever ridden in that manner."

one of the spirals. You've heard all the terms before: rag-dolling, rinse cycle, ad infinitum. But none of those terms really capture how fast you go from the surface to fifteen feet under. They also don't emphasize how alone you feel down there, and that no number of Jet Skis or water patrols can save you from a sound thrashing. When you're in the grips of one of these turbulence fingers, you're on your own.

7. If you have the confidence to ride it out, you'll stay relaxed, but a couple of things can chip away at that confidence when you're underwater. One, Maverick's is a multilayered reef, so there's the potential for a three- or four-tier wipeout. The turbulence can send you deep off the first reef, pick up momentum on the second shelf, and send you even deeper on the third and fourth. That's where the two-wave hold-downs come in. On this one, let's just say I got pushed into the second shelf and have a whole lot of swimming to do to get to the surface.

8. The other confidence killer is the dreaded leash. Sometimes, it's a lifesaver, because you can literally climb it to the surface. Other times, it's a death trap, especially when your board's tombstoning and you're being pulled in an opposite direction—usually straight down. It's impossible to surface and impossible to get to your leash, which will send shivers of panic through even the soundest water-men. I have a good pull during my beating, but I'm able to free myself from that underwater current and get out of there.

9. Back at the surface, I'm not out of the wilderness yet. A wipeout on the bowl usually means you're taking a couple more on the head. And depending on how far in you went, Sail Rock and its handful of jagged, mussel-encrusted brothers become an issue. In this case, I'm swimming sideways toward the channel as fast as I can and diving deep as each new white water approaches.

10. If you're going through the rocks, it's best to take off your leash and let your board go. Too many surfers have had their leashes wrap around rocks and get stuck there, held underwater. I've some-how made it out of harm's way here and, with nothing more than a slight headache, I shake it off and paddle back out to the peak. What

are the long-term effects of yet another sound beating? As Gerry Lopez once said about wipeouts at Pipeline, "I died just a little bit."

Surfers have been eating it at Mav's for fifteen years now, but some will always be etched in our minds. The late, great Jay Moriarity's 1994 crucifix wipeout remains as vivid as if it happened this morning: Jay paddling out, fresh off a boat. A handful of us, huddled around the peak, voicing our worries about the offshore winds and the massive swell. Jay flipping around on the first set he sees, me yelling, "Good night, Jay!" and then hearing the blood-curdling screams from the line of surfers on the shoulder. "Oh my Gooooooodd!" If big-wave wipeouts didn't have a poster child before then, they certainly found one in young Jay. He broke his board on that wave, but grabbed his backup and was back out there charging within fifteen minutes.

A lot of Mav's surfers say their worst beatings occur on the smaller days or when they least expect it, which could explain Mark Foo's tragic fall. It was an ordinary-looking wave and an ordinary-looking wipeout, but maybe that's the point: There's nothing ordinary about Maverick's. For all we know, that wave could have involved five tiers of turbulence.

More recently, Santa Cruz surfer Mike Brumett's biff during the 2005 contest deserved a ten if the judges knew anything about high-diving. Straight from the apex of the peak, Brumett never got to his feet as he launched way out there, hitting the flats in sync with the lip. The brunt of the impact was enough to make him cough up blood.

Personally, I've had a number of serious ones. One of those falling lips I mentioned completely blew out my knee in '99, requiring surgery and forcing me to question my motivation for riding big waves. I spent a lot of time on the sidelines, wondering if I really wanted to surf Maverick's again. But when I did, I felt like I was right back in the game. I took my share of terrible wipeouts, and that was just fine, too. As any dedicated Mav's surfer will probably tell you, wipeouts are necessary. They remind you how good it feels to make one of those damn things.

ALISTAIR CRAFT ON A TOW-IN CURTAIN
CALL THAT DEPOSITED HIM ON THE ROCKS.
BROKEN SKI, BROKEN BOARD, BROKEN EGO.

BEING FLEA

64

BRUCE JENKINS

"If you panic, you die."
—test pilot Chuck Yeager

In a riveting scene from the film *The Right Stuff*, Chuck Yeager comes back from the dead. Spinning out of control in his NF-104 aircraft, circa 1963, Yeager gets ejected by parachute at 7,000 feet. The experience is brutal, leaving him with multiple injuries and severe burns. But Yeager (played by Sam Shepard) gets to his feet and walks away, through the smoke. The man who would not die.

Personality differences aside, Flea Virostko is the Chuck Yeager of surfing. He has the most guts *and* talent to burn. He attempts things most surfers wouldn't even consider, and once immersed in the commitment, he becomes a master of his craft—and of survival. There is no panic in Flea, and he has spent a lifetime emerging from hell.

Where do you start with Flea? With his victories in the first three Maverick's contests? With his tow-in mission through the pit of a 70-foot face? With his life-threatening ordeal on the rocks? With a Jet

FLEA VIROSTKO, DECEMBER 22, 2000. EVEN MIKE PARSONS, WHO WON THAT YEAR'S BILLABONG XXL AWARD, CALLED IT "THE HEAVIEST WAVE OF THE WINTER."

GRANT WASHBURN: "The one time I tried to tow, I wiped out and came up to watch the biggest wave I've ever seen break right in front of me. Once I came up from that, I figured nothing could hurt me, but I was heading straight for the rocks. I couldn't see Jeff, who'd towed me in, but all of a sudden there's Flea, just driving around. He's more gung-ho than anybody about going into the pit and rescuing a guy. I thought, 'Of course it's Flea. Who else would be crazy enough to come in here?' It was cool. I got him a case of beer."

Ski rescue attempt so borderline, he got mowed down by a giant wave from behind?

Perhaps the essential Flea moment came during the 2004 Eddie Aikau contest, held in 25-foot surf that represented Waimea Bay's best day in years. With the great Bruce Irons backing off, yelling at Flea to go on a massive set wave, he went—straight into oblivion, freefalling some forty feet and injuring his knee so badly, he was unable to compete in the Maverick's contest three months later.

The point wasn't that Flea got hurt, but that he went. Flea Would Go. And the question comes to mind: What's it like being the most radical surfer? With everyone expecting an Evel Knievel performance, does he *have* to go? Does part of him yearn for a more conventional reputation?

Not likely. Not after some fifteen years charging big waves around the world. "I don't look at a wave and figure, that's too big, or that's big enough," he says. "I just go. I'd do it for free. In fact, I'd pay to go do it."

Flea presents a hard-edged, distrustful attitude to anyone outside his inner circle on the West Side of Santa Cruz. Looking wary and bored, he gives clipped answers in most every interview. "Shit, you can't be nice to everyone," he once told *Surfer* magazine. "Sometimes, I just want to be a dickhead."

It seems that's a bit of a tradition in Flea's world. Bully-style enforcement became a necessary evil once Santa Cruz's most popular surf spots became overcrowded. Vince Collier, Anthony Ruffo, and friends were heavy influences on the young Flea, a diminutive kid (thus the nickname) who knew he'd have to be aggressive to make his mark.

"When we first started surfing Maverick's in the early '90s," says Matt Ambrose, "I remember showing up on the cliff one day and seeing this little guy drop in, do the craziest bottom turn, and get into the pocket, just carving under the lip. I knew who it was. We were all competitive from the youth contests back then. And I remember just being sick to my stomach watching him go off."

"The whole thing is, he's top-heavy," says Shawn Rhodes, "so his balance, center of gravity, and paddling power are really good. I noticed him when he was just a little grommet, surfing against him in contests. I beat him a lot back then, but now, he's kind of unstoppable. And you could always see it in him. The little guy who wanted to prove something."

As longtime friend Josh Loya remembers it, "He got things done by being super radical. When we were growing up, the Santa Cruz kids ahead of us were pretty wild. They'd steal your bike, try to hump your sister, stuff like that, and they're like thirteen at the time. They were terrorizers. If you had a new bike and they wanted it, they'd just take it for a week, bend the tires, then bring it back: 'Aw, that bike sucked.' If you were the new kid surfing the Lane, they'd take your towel off while you were changing. They'd whip you with kelp. Those were Flea's role models. If you're kind of leaning that way in the first place, that stuff's gonna rub off on you.

"There was a thing called 'hellgie beatings,'" says Loya. "Little groms were called Hellgromytes, and the idea was to slap 'em around, give 'em charley horses, just because they're kids. Flea's always been into that. Kids like him and respect him, even after he punches 'em in the leg and gives 'em a big bruise. Because he's Flea. He's not doing it to be a jerk, just because it happened to him, so why shouldn't it happen to the next kid? If he doesn't, how are they gonna know to pass it on [laughter]?"

Slap fights are big among Flea's adult contemporaries. "After many Budweisers, we really go at it," Flea told videographer Eric W. Nelson a few years back. "Me and my friends, Vince Collier and the guys, just thrashing each other for fun." Flea was shirtless during the interview, with a huge bandage wrapped across his torso. "My friend Paul really landed a solid one," he said. "Broke one of my ribs. That's when the fun ended."

It seems that the whole rowdy package is fun for Flea, which pretty much explains everything. "You wonder who's writing the scripts for him," says Loya, jokingly. "He couldn't come up with this stuff on his own. But that's how his mind works. He doesn't think the way normal people do. Nothing's planned out. He goes more on instinct, like that wave at the Aikau, and he can be just as radical on land. He's not gonna rob a bank or anything like that, but he does stuff and then thinks about it later."

Several years ago, says Loya, the boys were checking the surf at a spot north of Santa Cruz. "A neighbor of Flea's dad was out there with a Volvo station wagon," said Loya. "The surf didn't look any good, so Flea jumps into his truck, peels out through the lot, and has no idea that he's spraying this guy's car with rocks. Flea's lucky the guy was level headed, but I mean, he broke one of the guy's windows. He got all sorry and offered to pay for it, but that's Flea—he does stuff because it's fun, but without thinking that it might not be cool.

"I've talked to him about it," Loya goes on. "He says, 'It's like I *have* to do these things, but I don't feel any pressure to be radical.

BETTER THAT FLEA VIROSTKO ISN'T LOOKING
BEHIND HIM. HE WOULDN'T WANT TO KNOW.

FLEA VIROSTKO: "I hate to say it, but the truth is Maverick's is a heavier wave than Waimea. It has the freezing-ass water, sharks, and it's more top-to-bottom down the line. If you take off deep enough, your problems just start when you get to the bottom. There's a long wall and an inside bowl that can drill you and send you right into the rocks. I've gone down hard at Waimea, but it's pretty much just a drop."

It's just what I do.' That's the way people think of Flea, and that *is* him. He didn't turn around and go at the Eddie to get a magazine cover, or because he thought he'd lose sponsorship money if he didn't. It just seemed like the obvious decision to him, whether it was gonna work or not."

Heavy partying is another West Side tradition, and Flea seldom leaves much to the imagination. None of the crew gives much in the way of detail, but Kenny Collins says, "West Side parties get pretty deep. Kind of like the Rolling Stones would do, times ten. Makes Keith Richards look like a Boy Scout. Some people have to run away and hide, including myself."

As a result, Flea has surfed more than a few big swells with a major hangover. Not that you'd notice. "In my mind, Flea is pretty calculating," insists Zach Wormhoudt. "He always knows what he's doing. He's not just pickled from the night before, going late because he's in a stupor. He's on it. He's not some Jeff Spicoli who happens to ride big waves."

That became evident in the first three Maverick's contests, when Flea consistently stepped to the plate and knocked a tape-measure home run. "I think he's been a lucky bastard in the contests, but I can't really take anything away from the guy," says Rhodes. "First he takes out Richard Schmidt, champion of all NorCal big waves. Then in the second contest he takes out Kelly Slater, the best surfer in the world. That's earning it."

Perhaps the most notable also-ran, however, is Peter Mel. As radically as Flea charges Maverick's, Mel has an even stronger reputation among his peers. Many found it shocking that Mel finished behind Flea in all of those contests. "Flea's just driven," says Mel. "And every time I'm with him, he seems to be more driven. To him, rivalry is a front-burner thing. He doesn't say it, but he wants to beat me bad. Probably because I get a lot of press, all that blah-blah about being 'the man' out here. But he's a spiteful little guy. He does not like having that label go to someone else."

PETER MEL (LEFT) AND FLEA VIROSTKO, TAKING
THEIR RIVALRY TO THE BIGGEST STAGE.

The pressurized Maverick's theater has created a love-hate relationship between Flea and Mel. Just as they'll jab each other over bragging rights, it is an association built on deep respect. "Guys like Peter and Richie [Schmidt] are my biggest influences in the water," says Flea. "Guys who take off and aren't afraid and like to go for it. Sometimes I think Pete's a little bit fuckin' crazy, but he knows what he's doing. He pushes me. He gets underneath that hook and catches it real quick, where I'm a little slower to get down and I get air-drops. I generally don't worry about what anybody else is doing or saying, but Pete impresses me. If people think he's Mister Maverick's, I don't really agree. And I don't feel I have that much to prove."

Most Maverick's surfers have a difficult time isolating Flea as king of the break. "You can't say that," Rhodes agrees. "Based on the sessions I've watched over the years, Jeff Clark is the top dog, with Grant, Peter, Evan, Ambrose, and Flea in a group right behind him. I've just seen Jeff take too many giant waves, way too often, with nothing riding on it. First wave of the set, he doesn't care; he's not afraid to die. Even when he goes out there hurt, which is often, he's an absolute badass."

There are times when Flea looks like anything but a madman. He suffers from asthma, a hellish development for someone intent on riding 35-foot surf. "I can relate to that, having asthma myself," says Mark Renneker. "Flea carries a little 'puffer' to provide medication if he really needs it, but he rarely lets people see him inhale from it, probably in keeping with the tough-guy image he wants to portray. But I remember after he won the first Maverick's contest, he had this goofy hairstyle and people were making fun of him on the TV news. He finally revealed that he'd worn his hair that way as a show of solidarity to a friend who had cancer. I give him a ton of credit for breaking from the mold. For being human."

When Flea got caught inside during a huge swell in 1998, his aura of invincibility was gone. Left with only the tail of his board, he had to deal with the 20-foot leash still attached to it. Videos captured his harrowing episode on the rocks, trapped by his equipment as the leash got tangled. Months later, he revealed the gravity of the situation: "I was already completely worked by getting sucked over the falls of a giant, pitting wave. So now I'm right in by the rocks, trying to swim to the other half of my board, just so I could get up on it and puke a little bit. But there was no way. I figured my leash would break, but it didn't. I couldn't get the thing off, and I was just getting thrashed on the rocks. That was, like, six or seven waves. I'd barely get to the surface, and another white-water would drive me right back down, like a fat woman sitting on my face. Almost died. Finally I got the leash off and swam into the lagoon. It was pretty heavy. I was out of there after that. Didn't want to see no more."

"That's the thing about Flea," says Washburn. "If you get him in a quiet moment, he can be this nice, mellow guy, and he'll talk about things. It's just that first instinct, the need to be Flea. When he showed up for the '05 Maverick's contest, unable to surf because of the knee injury, a TV crew interviewed him. And he goes, 'Aw, this is bullshit. If it were real Maverick's, I would have surfed it.' He actually said that. But it's not what he meant. He was totally bummed that he couldn't surf, and the only thing he could rationalize was that the surf wasn't that good. And of course, we had some 25-foot sets and very real Maverick's that day. He was smart enough not to go; he just wasn't honest enough with himself to give the real reason."

On a big-wave expedition to South Africa in the summer of 2005, featuring several of the world's top riders, Washburn caught some rare glimpses of Flea. "I've never seen a guy help so many people on an airplane," he says. "Usually when a flight is boarding, everyone's into his own thing. I was sitting there trying to fathom a seventeen-hour flight where I'm too big (6'6") for my seat. Flea stood in the aisle helping ladies get their bags in the bins, just one after another. He really went out of his way to do that.

"Once we got to Cape Town, we were confronted with inconceivable poverty. Most of us got sort of numb to it, but Flea was amazingly sensitive to the sight of down-and-out people on the street. It would have been easy for him to put on his headphones and just tune it all out, but he couldn't bear to walk by someone without offering a bit of money. I see things like that and I realize that Flea's critics should rethink their position on him."

John Raymond has watched Flea's escapades from the early days at Maverick's, and he doesn't quite see a takeover by the so-called Young Guns (Anthony Tashnick, Greg Long, Ryan Augenstein, Russell and Tyler Smith) just yet. "I don't think they're anywhere near as good as Flea," says Raymond. "But I'm worried about him in the long haul. What is he, thirty-three? As he gets older, he's going to fight that decline tooth and nail, and he'll have trouble dealing with that. There will be a new Flea, and that's going to bug him, too. He's going to want to kill this new Flea, and he's going to go deeper than the new Flea, but he's going to be forty years old and maybe it won't be the same. I think the aging process will be a little harder on him than most of us."

One of the true tests of a surfer's longevity is his ability to recover, both mentally and physically, from a life-and-death crisis. Kimo Hollinger, a fearless Waimea rider, didn't surf anywhere for several years after an incident on the inside rocks that nearly killed him. Cody Graham, who hit the water with Todd Chesser on the day Chesser died at Outside Alligators, hasn't been the same big-wave surfer since that day. Loya, Evan Slater, and Jake Wormhoudt endured Maverick's wipeouts that left cobwebs in their confidence. Kenny Collins went to Jaws, surfed an epic day with Laird Hamilton and the Maui crew, and took a wipeout so severe he swore off big-wave riding for a while. Mike Parsons nearly died at Maverick's in December '94 (in the same set of waves that killed Mark Foo), and he has not returned as a paddle-surfer.

Flea, while showing the occasional glimpse of vulnerability, is the man who keeps coming back. His bravado was never more evident than the December 22, 2000, swell that brought 35-foot, island-style surf to Maverick's. Parsons won the XXL big-wave cash award that year, for a bomb he scored at Cortes Bank, but most everyone agreed that Flea's signature wave was beyond extreme. As Washburn recalls, "On a face that had to be 70 feet, just throwing hollow like a cartoon, Flea faded into the deepest spot, pulled into this giant barrel and barely, barely escaped with his life. To me, it couldn't have been more serious. It was the most radical surf you've ever seen, and Flea's wave was the heaviest I'd ever seen. It was like something from a different planet. Everyone had been towing around, riding the shoulder, and here comes this guy just fading, fading, impossibly deep on a huge wall of water, knowing that it's gonna break ahead of him in the bowl. When he pulled up and went across, I thought he'd doomed himself. I think he escaped because it broke so hard. He outran the barrel because it was so vicious. It got him in the end, though. It was shocking. After ten years of watching these waves, it was shocking to see that."

Then there was the 2000 Maverick's contest, the most challenging to date with its consistent 20-to-25-foot surf and a semifinal heat (Flea, Ambrose, Moriarity, Washburn, Collins, Kelly Slater) that ranks with the most spectacular ever held in a paddle-surf contest. Flea spent that entire day charging, wave after wave, heat after heat, taking the occasional frightful wipeout between high-scoring rides. "Flea . . . dude, that guy's a piece of work," Slater said at the after-party. "I've been all over the world and surfed a lot of big-wave spots. This guy was turning around and going on waves that only a handful of guys in the world would want."

The definitive moment came at the start of the final. With a full day of manic behavior in his wake, Flea went down hard on his very first takeoff. "It was just ridiculous," says veteran big-wave surfer Steve Dwyer, who was watching from the channel. "He spun on his back three times and went down as hard as you possibly can. If that's me, my day's over. But this guy, when he headed back out, I could see the water pulling off his hands, and he was paddling the way most guys would after a career wave. Right then, I knew he'd win. Flea's a bit rude of a personality, but fuck, can he surf."

THE MAVERICK'S ELITE, AS ONLY SANTA CRUZ CAN BRING IT (FROM LEFT TO RIGHT): JOSH LOYA, FLEA VIROSTKO, AND RICHARD SCHMIDT.

DOUG ACTON: "This was taken during the infamous '100-foot swell' in November 2001, some of the most extreme shooting conditions I've ever experienced. Clouds, rain, winds from all directions—Mother Nature threw it all our way. I was down to my backup camera, with only eight shots left, when this bomb started feathering. I used up the roll on this Flea Virostko wave, then got the distinct feeling I had to get out of there. Heading in, I felt for the first time that any kind of mistake could be my last. There were no breaks between sets, cutting off all the normal routes. When I rounded Mushroom Rock, I had to negotiate two feet of foam covering the entire inner reef. It was insane. It never felt so good to get back to the dock and touch dry land."

TRAGEDY REVISITED

GRANT WASHBURN

My mother was there on the landing, hands wringing the rail, and as she spoke my name, I was flushed by a feeling of dread. I knew something horrible had happened.

"Doc Renneker just called. Mark Foo died today surfing at Maverick's," she said. And she started to cry.

She didn't know Foo, but she knew he had drowned with my friends, doing what I loved to do. She knew I had surfed Maverick's all week, that I'd changed flights to the East Coast so I could surf it some more. She had never truly liked big-wave riding, and now her worst fears had been confirmed.

It was as if the cold lip of a 20-foot wave had crashed right through the door of my parents' Florida home. The fact that someone had died surfing Maverick's was a shock, but not surprising. That it was Foo, one of the most experienced and prepared athletes

MARK FOO SEQUENCE, DECEMBER 23, 1994.
THE LAST WAVE OF HIS LIFE.

MARK RENNEKER: "Foo and Ken Bradshaw came over together, flew all night, landed at 6 A.M., came to my house a little after 7. Kenny was totally energized, fully stoked, the old Kenny. Foo stayed in the back seat of the rental car, crumpled up like some refugee. He looked tired, like he was trying to collect himself. When we changed in the parking lot, Mark was really tentative. He had a lot of questions."

in the sport, was hard to grasp. He was one of the best, and that left us all more vulnerable than we had hoped.

The manner and cause of his death was—and is—of great importance to us. A number of theories were documented: He was hit on the head . . . his leash got caught on the bottom . . . too much travel, not enough sleep, a wetsuit too thin. I think a lot of surfers clung to the notion that he suffered a concussion, until the autopsy ruled that one out. It's like people needed to justify how he died, ideally in a manner so unusual that they'd feel better about their own chances out there.

To this day—a full twelve years after the fact—I don't think we've heard the proper explanation. I think Mark Foo was killed by the sheer power of Maverick's, in deceptively dangerous conditions, with no complications beyond the simple fate of drowning.

All accounts suggest that December 23, 1994, was a "small" day at Maverick's, but it definitely was not. This was a long-period swell, with 20-second intervals, making conditions doubly life-threatening. It was a day of thick, fast-moving walls and multiple-wave sets. The ferocity of a wipeout on such days is not well represented by photos, as people who ride these waves know. Foo's fall was similarly downplayed. It was unspectacular when compared to other wipeouts of the historic week, particularly the absurd plunge that landed Jay Moriarity on magazine covers around the globe. But something struck me while reviewing the footage with Evan Slater.

Like coaches sifting through game films, we scrutinized the session. We watched a Slater freefall that didn't seem too bad—especially for him—except that "I thought I broke my ribs on that one," he recalled. "Knocked the wind out of me, bad." Then we watched Foo's fateful wave, another midface splat, and suddenly the impact became more pronounced. If Slater felt he'd crushed his ribs, Foo might have felt something worse. Over and over we watched him slap into the face, *whop*! It must have been like being kicked in the gut by an elephant. And then he went up and over, hard.

RICHARD SCHMIDT: "I knew it wasn't going to be easy for those guys to just jump straight into Maverick's. I've been coming back to California for years after entire winters in Hawaii, and you can't just throw on a wetsuit and be 100 percent the first time. Foo was an awesome athlete, though, and I was completely shocked when I heard what happened. In those early years, guys with no big-wave experience were taking some really bad wipeouts and surviving. To have a guy like Mark pass away, that didn't make sense to me."

Even if Foo got a good breath, and the initial impact hadn't knocked the wind out of him, the trip over the falls would have been rough. Long-period intervals factor into the equation in exponentially heavy increments, and this was extreme. The concussion of the lip can be devastating, and when a surfer is launched over the barrel and driven into the pit, he will likely be given as intense a thrashing as the wave can deliver—and then he will be sucked into "the trench," a deep-water spot shoreward of the reef's pinnacle. This is where most of the two-wave hold-downs occur. Surfers sucked over the falls are nearly guaranteed a visit to the black depths of the trench.

It's a spooky place. During the summer of 2002, Matt Ambrose and a photographer went scuba diving in that area. They found no cracks or "fingers" of reef that might snag a leash beneath the main peak. In fact, Ambrose said he was relieved when he saw what made the main bowl plunge, as it was a smooth, undersea mound. But he was quite disturbed by the dark trench that lay beneath it.

Three years after Foo's death, Neil Matthies wiped out at Maverick's on a monstrous peak. I was at the end of the cliff, filming the session, and watched in horror at what appeared to be a certain fatality. Matthies was sucked up and over the falls, and then deposited deep in the impact zone. An even larger wave approached as the spray cleared, but there was no sign of Matthies. As the second wave began to break, we caught the terrifying glimpse of his board "tombstoning"—pointing straight at the sky—meaning Matthies was at least 20 feet (the length of his leash) below the surface.

It's a curious sensation to be yanked upward by your foot while the water around you is draining to the depths. In those harrowing moments, I've always been relieved that something is trying to keep me near the surface, and frightened by just how deep I might be if not tied to a massive chunk of foam. You're essentially stuck in this position, but you know that if you release your leash, you'll go even farther down.

The next wave landed on his tombstoning board and swept it toward the rocks. For Matthies to stay under for that second wave, with his breath and confidence expiring, was an unbelievable test of endurance and will. He finally surfaced a full 45 seconds after the initial impact, having traveled more than 100 yards inside the trench. Had his board been shattered like Foo's, he might still be down there. It is obvious, viewing after viewing, that he was lucky to escape with some cracked vertebrae.

As we watch the footage of Foo's wipeout, we know several things for certain. His leash was attached to a tiny chunk of surfboard that offered him little buoyancy. He didn't clear the trench before he bumped into Mike Parsons, who had wiped out on the following wave. There were several more waves in the set. Parsons, still attached to his large board, was quickly washed onto the rocks. Foo had been deeper than Parsons, and as several camera angles confirm, he did not surface before the third wave. If he hadn't been able to get a good breath, or had the wind knocked out of him, Foo may have blacked out before he hit Parsons. If he was still holding out, it's likely that he lost consciousness under the third wave. A minute after he went down, the set was still booming.

Might another surfer have escaped? If he hadn't been wearing a leash, would Foo still be alive? Did the tail of his board get mangled by rocks deep beneath the bowl? Having ridden Maverick's many hundreds of times, and having encountered the raw power of such scenarios, I find these arguments misguided. I believe that fitness and gear played minimal roles, and I think we're doing a disservice to future generations by clinging to a theory of "unlucky" entanglement. A person washed through the inside is virtually guaranteed to encounter rocks, and that would explain the mangled board. I believe that even the most prepared surfer in the world can be held down for an eternity at Maverick's. It seems entirely plausible to me that Foo simply drowned. In fact, there is little evidence to suggest otherwise.

"The cold water's just so heavy. You're under for two seconds, you get the ice-cream headache, and you can't even see straight. I came to Hawaii thirty years ago to get away from that. Hey, if you park by the church at Waimea and time it right on the sets, you can be in the lineup seven minutes after you got out of your car. At Sunset you don't even have to paddle; the rip takes you out, and the waves take you in. We're in Jacuzzi Land over here." — CHARLIE WALKER

THE VIEW FROM HAWAII

Hawaiians have made only fleeting appearances at Maverick's, both before and after Mark Foo's death. Even as Half Moon Bay has become Hawaii's equal as a big-wave destination, the two remain worlds apart. The following is a view of Maverick's from some of Hawaii's most distinguished big-wave riders.

KEN BRADSHAW: Logistically, if you don't live there, it's a very difficult thing to do. There's the financial end, which has always been a problem for me, and also the emotional aspect—planning trips when part of you believes you should just stay in Hawaii and not go jet-setting around. It got to where I had to make some choices, and I haven't ridden the place at all since the late 1990s. There's so much politics surrounding the place—Santa Cruz guys, city guys, tow guys, paddle guys, pretty juvenile stuff—I could never find someone who consistently wanted to partner up with me.

Do I miss it? Hell, it's an exciting, incredible wave. Most places reach a certain size where they simply become unridable. At Maverick's, you just move out to the next peak. I'd love to have been

there in December of 2000, when Carlos Burle, Noah Johnson, and those guys rode that outer reef at 35-feet plus. That's the swell I wanted. I always knew that existed, and I wanted it badly.

What I don't miss is agonizing over what to do. Catch the swell here, then fly all night to California? Make a commitment to just spend two weeks over there? I mean, Maverick's is rustic surfing. It's like going up to the Sierras and building a log cabin in brutal weather, then picking your spots for snowboarding. Here in Hawaii [North Shore of Oahu], it's all sunny and beautiful, I just roll out the boat, drop it in the water, and head to the outer reefs. I'm happy right where I am.

BROCK LITTLE: I caught the next wave after Mark Foo's in '94. It almost killed two people—myself and Mike Parsons. In the days thereafter, the three of us who came over from Hawaii—Foo, Bradshaw, and myself—were ridiculed for pushing each other too hard. "You have to measure the place, show some caution," they said. "Don't make people do things they normally wouldn't." Listen, for most surfers, that's very good advice. Not for me. I live to go *nuts* in big surf. I'm out there to take chances, push things to the limit, be part of the heaviest shit that goes down. That's how you progress; that's how barriers get broken. Can you imagine the history of big-wave surfing if everyone sat out on the shoulder, playing the percent-ages, counting how many waves they made?

Foo had that famous line about being "willing to pay the ultimate price," and that totally goes for me. Parsons and I both had heavy experiences on the rocks, and I was willing to die right there. I also had the will to pull myself out of it. You're lucky if you can draw on past experience at a time like that, and my mind took me back to when I was 19, on a giant day at Waimea. I was caught inside with a broken leash, and here comes a seven-wave set, all top-to-bottom, 30-foot closeouts. Boom! Boom! Boom! By the fourth or fifth wave, I had reached that point where you just give up. And it would have been *so* easy to just die, in the blackness. It was actually relaxing to hang out there. But I got a shot of adrenalin, a harsh slap of mortality, knowing it was my only way out.

That's how it was at Maverick's that day. I was absolutely getting my ass kicked, but I remember thinking, "I am *not* going to die here. I'm not going to have this big deal about Brock Little dying at Maverick's." I went from a panic stage to full analyzation; I kept my wits about me, and I found that I actually enjoyed it. And I've always enjoyed coming back for the contests. I kind of like that extremist angle: having that cup of joe in the freezing cold while you check it

out, wearing the wetsuit, the incredible feeling when you leave the water. It's kind of cool—but only for a couple of weeks.

LAIRD HAMILTON: The only reason I'd even consider going to Maverick's is that I'd get tired of people saying I haven't been there, or I should go there. I don't think anything can beat the challenge we have at Peahi [Jaws] or the camaraderie I have with my friends here. If we had a winter that was missing Hawaii and just hammering somewhere else, it would be stupid for me to sit here and not do something about it. But I don't think there's any place better. There are places that are different, and good, but are they better? No. Hawaii is the mecca, the place where surfing came from.

The cold water has nothing to do with it. I love cold water. I'd probably be wearing the thinnest suit if I got to Maverick's, because I'm really warm-blooded and my metabolism just works that way. I go snowboarding with all these mountain guys, and I wear less clothes than they do. I was in Belgium one time in winter, and I bet some guy I could go in the water in my surf shorts. I don't know what the temperature was, but it was stupid stuff, like five or six degrees. The guy said he'd give me 500 bucks if I could stay in for five min-utes. I stayed for fourteen. Of course, I had hypothermia and my teeth were chattering for, like, four hours, but I did it.

I watch all these guys running around the world, trying to catch a big wave, and I'm thinking, you might get some good ones, but at the end of the day, I'd like to have it happen at my home break. I mean, Mark Foo got no sleep when he went to Maverick's. Maybe that means something. Ross Clarke-Jones showed up at Peahi one winter, looking like he hadn't slept in a week, and got hurt pretty bad [two broken ribs]. If I really wanted to surf Maverick's, I'd go over and stay for a month. Get to know the spot and the people and surf it as many days as possible.

I'd love to surf Maverick's like Peahi was for us in the beginning. Like when Jeff Clark had it all those years. Or the first guys towing it. They've got a lot more guys sitting there wanting to ride it now, plus the whole tow-versus-paddle controversy, which we don't have. We don't tow where people are paddling, period. We'll go someplace else, even if it's smaller or less perfect. Over there you've got guys that aren't gonna catch any waves, but they're going to go out there and paddle, anyway, like it's some rite of passage, just to experience it. They're going to sit there and try to act like they're doing it, and then get pissed off when guys are towing. I've got no tolerance for that.

DAN MOORE [after being towed into (at the time) the biggest wave ever ridden at Maverick's, March of '99]: I had some bad wipeouts that day. Got pretty well traumatized, too. I've taken some horrendous beatings at Jaws, all manner of things on the North Shore, but this is about the heaviest thing I've ever experienced. Let me tell you, I have so much respect for the guys that surf it all the time. They're polar bears.

DARRICK DOERNER: I can't understand this whole thing where you show up late the night before, charge it first thing the next morning, and then try to chase the swell somewhere else. No. We want to leave a good impression. We want to go over and have barbecues, eat salmon, drink beer, go over the conditions and the variations, work with the group of people like we do here. A bunch of Maverick's guys have come over. Jeff and Pete and their partners, Skinny and Flea, very cool guys, all of them. And they were a part of us, they ate lunch and dinner with us, drank beers and laughed with us. That's what we want.

Yeah, I'd love to bang into Maverick's, deep. Those guys in a sense are my heroes, because the elements they have to go through are severe. The guys who first paddled out there on their own, before the big crowds, that's impressive. Some of the wipeouts. . . no wonder there's so many people on the cliff. That's what they want to see, and they aren't disappointed. They are rare individuals to be in 5-mil wetsuits, 48-degree water, hoods, booties, gloves, and actually be out there standing on a board—that's phenomenal.

DENNIS GOUVEIA [of the Hawaiian water patrol]: You go out there and you're reduced to nothing. First, I can't hear 'cause of my helmet. Then there's the fog, so now I can't see. Pretty soon it's so cold, I can't feel anything. You lose all your senses.

DAVE KALAMA: Those guys are frickin' nuts. I couldn't do it. I've acclimated quite well to the warm water over here. And the way they just throw themselves into oblivion sometimes, it's unbelievable. I know there's a lot of thrill to paddle-surfing out there, just pushing yourself over the ledge, but the success rate just doesn't quite add up for me. I'd actually like to go and tow it sometime, as long as there's not too much drama surrounding it. Like some big deal about Laird and I being over there. If we could have it low-pro, go out and surf with some of the boys, not have it be this giant event, that would be great.

KEN BRADSHAW, ONE OF THE FEW HAWAIIANS TO FREQUENTLY VISIT MAVERICK'S, ON THE LAST WAVE OF THE SET THAT KILLED MARK FOO.

BROCK LITTLE IN PARTY MODE.

KEN BRADSHAW (RIGHT) WITH MEL PU'U OF THE HAWAIIAN WATER PATROL.

"Yeah, Maverick's, it's . . . it's not really fun." — **KELLY SLATER**

FEAR

JOSH LOYA

(A cut above most Maverick's surfers in terms of sheer talent and grace, Loya was once a world-ranked competitor on the professional tour. He has also dealt with significant fear issues, forcing him to make many compromises on land. Somehow, he has overcome those limitations in the water, where he has been a respected big-wave surfer since the late 1980s.)

I've had a serious fear of heights since childhood. It's a series of recurring nightmares, all pretty much the same. I'm on a cliff, or on top of a building, and I'm not secure—ready to fall. In my day-to-day life, I deal with it constantly. If you put me on the deck of a tall building, just to stand on the railing and look over, I couldn't do it. I'd feel like laying down on the ground and slowly crawling back inside, because if I'm standing, I'm going to fall. It's a horrible feeling that comes over me, like I'm in a cold sweat and about to throw up, and it's gotten worse over the years.

I don't know what it means, other than I have vertigo-like symptoms. It's all about looking over the edge and feeling totally helpless. I'm terrified of the cliff at Maverick's, where the photographers sit. As long as I can look straight out, I'm fine; it's looking over the edge that

CHRISTY DAVIS: "I've been out there when I looked at waves breaking so big and so hard, I almost got sick to my stomach. Waves you could put a lighthouse inside. You look through the tube and you can see all of Moss Beach on the other side. And I just sit there thinking, I don't ever, ever want to be in there. I don't know how you could live."

MATT AMBROSE: "Up to 18 feet, if it's 17-to-20-second intervals, you're scared, but it's doable. If it's 18-plus and a little bit thicker, out of the west with longer intervals, it gets insanely hollow like Teahupoo [Tahiti]. At that point it's not like, can I surf these waves? It's more like, can I survive the drop?"

DON CURRY: "I love fear. I thrive on it. But there are times at Maverick's when it overwhelms you. There was a day in '97 when I was out there for three hours, just me and Jay and one other guy. None of us even took off— not once—and I'll admit to being psyched out. I felt like I was seeing things that I shouldn't have. Things that were not meant to be seen that close by the human eye. I felt like God and the devil were right there, and it could go either way."

92

SHAWN RHODES: "I've been through a lot of beatings, I've taken sets on the head, been caught inside, just about everything, and I'm still here, so it's not *that* brutal. At least, that's what I like to tell myself the night before, when the swells are pounding the rock wall outside my house and the windows are rattling: *"It's not that brutal, it's not that brutal . . ."*

gets me. Believe me, it's not fun.

Back around '94–'95, I had to quit snowboarding because of it. I could never handle the chairlifts to begin with. I'd have to close my eyes and have someone tap me on the shoulder when it was time to get off. But this one time at Kirkwood, a helicopter came looking for some guys who'd gotten lost on the mountain. The thing flew down to parking-lot level, we couldn't find it for a moment, and all of a sudden it flew right up from under us—right under the lift. I got a sickening feeling I can't even describe. I actually started crying. That was it. I was done for the day, and you're lucky if you see me once a year in the mountains.

So people ask me: If I can't look over the edge of something critical, how can I surf big waves? I really don't understand, except that I've always felt more comfortable in the water than on land. If you take a big fall in the surf, it's not like a splat on hard ground. I've had five or six fishing boats over the years, and I have no problem running sixty miles out to catch albacore, all day long, by myself. In big waves, I've spent twenty years taking big, nasty drops. Why I could do one edgy thing and be so scared of the others, I have no idea.

I was scared my first time out at Steamer Lane, when I was ten, but by the time I was twelve or thirteen, I was surfing serious waves all along the coast. I spent plenty of time in Hawaii, surfing Waimea and big Sunset. I first surfed Maverick's in 1992, and to this day, I've never had a session out there where I didn't catch a wave. So it's not like every big-wave session is some sort of test. I feel totally at ease out there. If I look over the edge of a wave and pull back, it's not that I'm freaked out. I do it for the same reasons anyone else would—feeling I was a little bit late, or the wave was going to close out, whatever.

There's this thing doctors talk about called the Young Man's Immortality Syndrome, a feeling that you're invincible. I was sort of in that zone over my first five years at Maverick's. I never took a bad wipeout. I was making all of my really critical drops. I wasn't taking big-time chances, but I wasn't being overly cautious, either. And I'd

94

IT'S NOT SO MUCH THIS WAVE HE'S WORRIED ABOUT, BUT THE NEXT ONE—OR FIVE.

GRANT WASHBURN: "The worst thing that can happen is a ten-wave set, five feet bigger than anything you've seen that whole day. You're right on the pulse of the Pacific Ocean, and whatever happened five days ago between the Aleutian Islands and Hawaii is about to unload on you. And you're sitting in the absolute worst possible place if a larger one comes in. Lots of guys surf big waves down in Santa Cruz, but if you're not used to having a 30-foot face go hollow and break right on top of you, you're not going to survive a ten-wave set."

still catch ten, fifteen good waves a day. Maybe I wasn't getting air-drops, but I was riding big waves and making them.

In November of 1997, a really heavy Maverick's day came along. It was 25 feet, easy, with a northeasterly wind and lumpy conditions. One of the heaviest days anyone had tried to paddle-surf at that time. Nobody got a solid ride and really completed it. Some pretty good surfers had to turn around and come in, without even catching a wave, after trying two or three times to penetrate the inside white-water. Guys like Jeff Clark and Richard Schmidt weren't even going out; didn't like the looks of it. But I was on a roll. I was just ahead of Zach Wormhoudt on the paddle-out, and while he got worked for about fifteen minutes, I made it out there with dry hair. I remember actually boasting about it: "My hair's dry!"

That was the last stupid thing I said. I stroked into a wave and took the beating of my life. I got to the bottom when my front foot started sliding—new booties, not scuffed-up enough to get good traction. Before I knew it, I was looking at a boat [in the channel] upside down. I wasn't down that long, but I really torqued my right knee and got rag-dolled so bad, it was the heaviest experience I'd had in surfing. The injury kept me out of the water for two months, and I didn't surf Maverick's again the rest of that season.

When I got back to Mav's the following year, I could tell that something wasn't right, that I didn't have the same mental outlook. An incredible set of giant waves came through and it kind of shell-shocked all of us, like we couldn't believe what we were seeing. We all kind of sat there, off to the side, wondering what the hell we were doing out there. It was probably like the feeling a NASCAR driver gets after a bad crash into the wall. Next time out, you're going to have some mental issues. But I worked my way through that. I caught a wave, rode it in, and had some really satisfying sessions after that. There was a day in December of '04 when Skinny [Collins] and I were up there, with our tow equipment, and I told him, "Let's do it the old way. We never used to have a ski. We used to just park in the lot, walk down the trail, and paddle out." That sounded cool enough to him, and we both went out and surfed a bunch of big waves.

That's the kind of thing that can build up your confidence for a long time.

Fear, to me, is driving up the coast to Maverick's, seeing nothing but whitewash at places you like to surf, and knowing you still have forty minutes to think about it. It's paddling for the wrong wave, turning around, and seeing a bigger wave that you're not going to get under. Going through the rocks, that's fear. But the worst is being held down to the point of giving up. I've had that—feeling that second wave go over you. You're almost to the top, and all of a sudden you're back in the spin cycle, head over heels again. That's bad, and at that point, the fear becomes panic. We all know that panicking is the worst thing you can do, but I think in that worst-case situation, where you're going limp and feeling like it's over, it can help you. It gives you a jolt of adrenaline and the will to snap out of it. This isn't the end. You freak out underwater, and you'll get to the top no matter what it takes.

I really don't know what kind of person I'd be if I didn't have the ocean. I just know that when I come in from a good session, especially in big waves, it's the best feeling in the world. Surviving a life-or-death crisis gives you confidence not just for the next time, but for a lot of scenarios you face in life. I've come to realize that I'm an above-average person in a traumatic situation. I've gained a ton of insight into my own mind, and what my body can handle. It has been my salvation.

97

"I started towing after that giant October '99 swell. A bunch of us tried to paddle out that day. We got washed all the way down to Blackhand, crazy current, paddled for our lives to get back to the jetty, barely got there, then got smashed against the rocks down there. Just totally bitch-slapped, basically. We went up on the cliff and watched Mel towing into giant waves, so easily, just turning off the lip and fading at the bottom. I looked at Ambrose and said, 'Time to get a Ski.'" — SHAWN RHODES

EVOLUTION REVOLUTION

PETER MEL

(Peter Mel is the master of Maverick's. For all the skill and bravado displayed by other surfers, none can match his precise, flowing interpretation of the art. He was considered the most talented paddle-in surfer throughout the '90s, executing more Maverick's tube rides and radical cutbacks than anyone else, and little has changed since Mel embraced the tow-in era. Somehow, major titles and cash awards have eluded him. The truth is in his performance, swell after swell.)

Big-wave surfing went nearly forty years without radical change. Whether it was Greg Noll and the boys at Waimea Bay or the huge swells of Maverick's in the early '90s, it was all about big boards, big drops, and pure survival. "Performance" was little more than being able to crank a bottom turn and make the wave without getting obliterated.

Then in '92 came tow-surfing, one of the most radical shifts in the history of any sport. It was a quantum leap, a method of wave riding that seemed almost surreal. For most of us, life was never the same.

It took me a while to really get involved in tow-surfing, which is

PETER MEL ON THE FIRST GIANT TOW-IN DAY AT
MAVERICK'S, OCTOBER 1999. SURFERS ON THE CLIFF
COULDN'T BELIEVE WHAT THEY WERE WATCHING.

TOWING IN ITS INFANCY: JIM KIBBLEWHITE BEHIND PETE McGLOTHLIN'S BOAT, SPRING OF 1994. AT THE TIME, KEN BRADSHAW AND JEFF CLARK WERE AMONG THOSE WHO RIDICULED THE IDEA.

BARNEY "AQUA MAN" BARRON, USING HIS SUPER TOW-IN POWERS.

"THE CONDOR," PETER MEL, SPREADING HIS WINGS.

funny, because I personally witnessed the breakthrough events. I was on the beach in '87 when they called off the Pipeline Masters and Herbie Fletcher took his Jet Ski out beyond the third reef to tow Michael Ho and Martin Potter into some bombs. I saw Potter S-turning along an unbroken wave, and when it started to pitch, he got an insane backside barrel and came out. I guess because it was such a sketchy, drizzly day, with hardly anyone around, people just forgot about it.

I also watched Laird Hamilton get the wave [in 1992] that really set the revolution in motion. He was at outside Backyards, attempting tow-ins with Darrick Doerner and Buzzy Kerbox, and I saw Laird get his historic ride all the way through Sunset. That was mental. Saw it with my own naked eyes. But I never really took it to another level, in my mind, until I saw the early videos of Laird and the "Strapped" guys at Jaws. That's when the light went on. And then I saw the Outside Log Cabins session on Big Wednesday [in January 1998] in Hawaii. That was the most mind-blowing of all.

To this day, it's the biggest clean surf ever ridden on the North Shore. Just the gnarliest day ever. I'd never even heard of the North Shore being closed out, but here were these huge, perfect waves way out to sea, and guys were towing in. I was staying at a friend's house on Ke Iki beach that winter. Ke Iki has to be the most insane shore-break in the world, and it was 25 feet island-style that day. But from the top of his house, we could see over it. We sat there with a case of beer and watched Ken Bradshaw, Noah Johnson, Ross Clarke-Jones, and a few other guys dropping into faces more than 60 feet high. That was the turning point. I told myself, "I'm buying a Ski," and as soon as I got back to Northern California, I did just that.

I bought it with no idea who I'd be towing with. I just knew I had to have one. I figured, "Buy boat, they will come." Originally I targeted Flea [Virostko], but he was traveling so much it wound up being Skinny [Collins]. But that turned out to be the perfect partnership. I've known Skinny my whole surfing career, going back to when I was twelve or thirteen, and we had something that clicked right off the bat.

My whole goal with the Jet Ski was to catch the biggest waves at Maverick's. I didn't think about anything else. What Laird and those guys were doing in Hawaii, I wanted to do here. We'd had some tow-ins at Maverick's already. Jim Kibblewhite was out there in the early '90s, and Vince Collier made a big impression with some tow-in excursions on relatively small days. And then, on the same huge swell I saw in Hawaii in '98, Perry Miller and Doug Hansen went out to

JEFF CLARK: FRESH LINES ON AN OLD PLAYING FIELD.

ONE OF SURFING'S GREAT NATURAL TALENTS, BARNEY
BARRON BECAME A TOW-IN STAR VIRTUALLY OVERNIGHT.

Maverick's on a windblown afternoon and caught a big one. Perry didn't make the wave; he couldn't really get off the bottom, and from what I understand, he really went down hard.

The truth is, I didn't really like that they were the first guys in the area to tow giant waves. Neither one of those guys had ever paddled into big surf—they just went straight to towing. I was thinking, wait a minute, Perry Miller? I mean, nice guy and all, but neither one of them paid any dues at Maverick's. So there was a big split between those guys and the thing I had going with Skinny.

October 28, 1999, was the day that changed our lives. It was Opening Day that season at Maverick's, and it just happened to be one of the two or three biggest swells we've ever seen there. It was kind of a gray, hazy morning, just off-the-scale huge, and nobody was even thinking of paddling out. But Skinny and I were on it, crack of dawn. We'd towed together quite a bit in the Santa Cruz area, and maybe three to five times at Maverick's the year before, and we had the basics down. The incredible part was that Jeff Clark and Grant Washburn [towing Clark, but not surfing] were the only other guys in the water. Biggest Maverick's waves anyone had ever seen, and we've got it all to ourselves.

People wonder how we pulled it off, with no past experience in that kind of size. I think it was just a scared-straight thing with us that day. In waves like that, you *have* to come through. You *can't* make mistakes, and we didn't. That's how we looked at it. We weren't holding back, either. Skinny stuck himself into a 50-foot barrel, easy, that day. So did Jeff. We plugged in to that day like it was made for us, the way it always seemed for Richie Schmidt and Jay Moriarity. We had gone to that next level in size. And at the very end, I dropped into this thing that wasn't even real, by far the biggest wave of my life. I've heard people say it was even bigger than the one Carlos Burle caught on the so-called "100-Foot Wednesday" [in November 2001], and I think it was, realistically.

Happiness isn't recognition, or a chunk of change. That stuff's nice, but the real satisfaction is being able to do it, just the *feeling* of it. You don't get that very often. When you've packed your stuff away and you're driving home, and your buddy's there, like Skinny and I heading back to Santa Cruz that day, and the buzz you feel right

KENNY COLLINS, EXPLORING PREVIOUSLY FORBIDDEN TERRITORY. NO WAY HE GETS THERE WITHOUT A SKI.

RICHARD SCHMIDT: "I think it's possible to paddle into a 30-footer, if you're in just the right spot. A lot of variables have to come together, but it's doable. It's just a lot more critical, a lot more risk. Myself, I'd rather ride a 25-, 30-foot wave on a tow board, because I'd feel handicapped on a 10-foot board. You can't put yourself where you want to be."

107

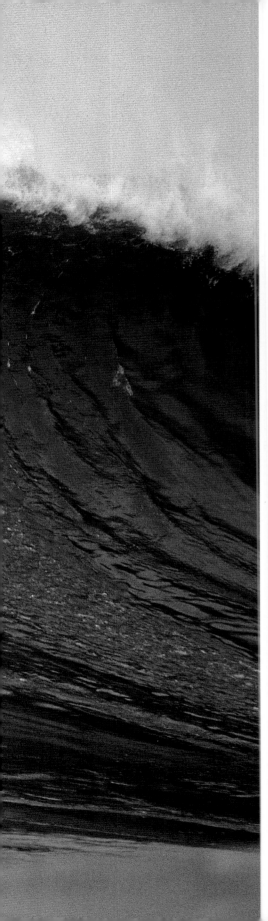

then—nothing tops that. That's what I strive for in life. Even at the age of thirty-six, I want it every swell, every year.

What's the best tow-in wave? I've surfed Jaws three times, and it's never been "real" Jaws, so I hesitate to compare it, but Jaws definitely moves a little quicker as an open-ocean setup, so it's more raw, not paddle-able at all. Guys have tried, and they're not getting anywhere near it. You've also got the wind, another big part of it. At Maverick's, things are slowed down a bit, you get more glassy days, and I just feel more comfortable in general.

Todos Santos [in Mexico] has a thinner lip and really stands tall, because of the bottom. Maverick's really has no back at all; it just jacks up insanely when it hits that reef. Todos is definitely just as dangerous because of the rocks inside, but it's not as powerful as Maverick's, not as dense, and by no means as long or as perfect.

Teahupoo [in Tahiti] is a whole different story. I was lucky to be one of the first guys to tow in there, and it's really dangerous. I watched a Jet Ski just get swallowed there. The thing stalled on the inside and literally disappeared. Gone. And this is in six feet of water. When it finally came up, it was destroyed beyond recognition. That's how radical the spot is, and you won't beat Teahupoo for a pure barrel. But I'm not a shallow-water guy. You can't do anything if you get slammed hard into the bottom. No expertise will help you, unless you're wearing body armor.

Cortes Bank [off the coast of California] is where the biggest waves will be ridden. It's out in the middle of the ocean, and it sits right on the continental shelf. But I like Maverick's better because of the consistency, and the weather. I've checked the Cortes conditions every swell, and nine times out of ten, the wind is blowing too hard. The other 10 percent of the time, it's not big enough or the swell direction's not quite right. So overall, I have to go with Maverick's. I've been to all of these places, and more, up and down the Pacific coast. I've searched as much as anyone. On a really good day, Maverick's is the best big wave in the world.

109

> "The whole thing about towing is having someone you can trust as a partner. Someone who wants to charge just as hard as you do. Someone who knows your capabilities, so you're exactly where you want to be when you let go of the rope. The kind of guy where you just *look* at each other, in a crisis, and there's total understanding."
> — JEFF CLARK

THE TOW TEAM

KENNY COLLINS

(Kenny "Skindog" Collins grew up on the West Side of Santa Cruz, where the standard of greatness is to rip waves of any size. At first, no one at Maverick's took him seriously. He seemed little more than a brash, loud-mouthed kid. Time has shown him to be one of the best surfers ever to ride the place, either paddling or towing. Far from irresponsible, he has become known for his smart decisions and winning attitude.)

I never planned to be a tow surfer. I didn't even want to do it until I heard from Peter Mel, who wasn't having success with anybody else. When he asked me, I was pretty flattered. That's something you don't really turn down. We started around '96 and around '98–'99 is when everything clicked in.

I'd much rather paddle-surf on a 20-foot glassy day with five of my friends than anything else in the world. But if it's 35-foot Maverick's, that's cut and dried. That's when I grab the rope and try to push surfing up a notch or two. It's either that or just sit there and watch, so there's no doubt which way I'm going.

Because of Pete, my surfing has improved immeasurably. He's one of the best in the world, so there's a lot of pressure. And Pete is

IN A SPORT THAT LEADS TO MANY DIFFERENT PARTNERSHIPS, KENNY COLLINS GOES IN AS JAY MORIARITY KICKS OUT. NOVEMBER 30, 2000.

KENNY COLLINS AND PETER MEL, THE FIRST GREAT TOW-IN TEAM AT MAVERICK'S.

NOVEMBER 1999: KELLY SLATER TOOK A BAD ONE ON HIS FIRST SESSION AT MAVERICK'S. JEFF CLARK GOES IN FOR THE PICKUP.

MATT AMBROSE: "I'm hoping we can adopt the rules they're setting up in Hawaii: If you want to be a tow-in guy, you have to meet a certain amount of criteria, get registered, pass a big-wave survival test. So you get a standard that will weed out all the goofy stuff. I don't like the idea of regulations, but I don't think there's any other way, because there are way too many cowboys. They just show up and don't give a shit about anything."

never, ever scared. It'll be 5:30 in the morning, still dark, and he's like, "Let's go! Get me into this next wave!" I like that. I end up going pretty hard as the day goes on, but he's just, bam! Right from the start. Pete and I had some incredible times there, especially that one October day (in 1999) when we had consistent 30-footers, just one after another, the biggest day I've ever seen.

Peter's last wave that day, I guarantee you, it's in the top five big waves ever surfed. That was a bowl we never even saw before. We were 200 yards past the regular bowl, and here comes this thing on the horizon. I thought it was gonna break on us, but it backed off just enough, and I did this huge U-turn and flung him into it. Just the gnarliest, ugliest wave ever surfed, and throwing out like 100 yards ahead of him. I was shitting bricks when I saw him take the drop. I thought I towed him right into death. But he got off the bottom, rode it perfectly, and when he kicked out of that thing he looked like he was on drugs, his eyes were so big. It was scary, but that was our mission, to catch the biggest wave. And that's Peter Mel. He wanted it.

If you're talking eight-foot beachbreak, I'll tow in with anybody if I know things are safe. But when you start taking it into Maverick's, or Jaws, or some secret spots up the coast, I probably wouldn't trust more than three people—Pete, Josh Loya, Adam Replogle. That's it. Guys I've worked with in huge waves before. Everybody's a little different. Adam's just snapping out there, so adamant about getting waves, and I never feel like I've done a good job until we get back to the beach and he relaxes a little bit. Josh is the kind of guy who'll get one or two phenomenal waves and be happy with that, and he'll tow you into eight. That's not a bad thing at all.

Your partner has to be someone who will put surfing big waves as a priority above wife, kids, family, job, the whole nine yards. That's a big commitment out of anybody, which is why guys have so much trouble finding people they can count on. Someone who will put you where you need to be on a wave, and who you know will come get you when you take one on the head.

JOSH LOYA (LEFT) AND
FLEA VIROSTKO, IN SYNC.

DOUG ACTON: "This was the day Kenny Collins discovered that towing and 10-foot paddle-boards don't mix. As soon as he let go of the rope, the board slowed down and the wave just mowed him. Lesson learned. He never made that mistake again." March 1999.

DEEPER BLUE

More and more crews are coming onto the scene, and there's a few kinks we need to work out. Like greed. It's kind of like getting a wave on a longboard; you're so pumped up, you don't even think about the other guys and you paddle right back out for the next wave. With towing, you might have some of the nicest people in the world, but behind the wheel they're just jerks, you know? That's what happens at Maverick's, guys cutting in line. In paddle-surfing, the best guys get the waves because they're the best. That means nothing in tow-surfing. The worst guy can get as good a wave as the best guy. And if they don't have any manners, things go a little haywire.

I think all of that's going to fade out in time. People are starting to realize that if you sit back for a second, you might get a big one that sneaks under everybody. We're getting more comfortable with the influx of so many guys from other countries, and I think it's going to get easier, more polite. I'd definitely like to see a limit placed on the number of teams out there at one time. If you're an out-of-towner going to Maverick's and there are ten local guys out there, don't even bother going out. Or go sit on the sidelines and wait for the coach to call you off the bench. As soon as you get five waves—including myself, Flea, and Barney, whoever it is—then go sit on the shoulder and let everyone else have a turn at it. I used to be all gnarly and territorial about it, but now I'm thinking, who am I to be the bad guy? I'm really careful who I call out now.

The one thing I'd like to see is some kind of rule where everybody has to paddle into 20-foot waves first, so you know what you're messing with. To be right in the bowl when a huge set comes. That'll teach you more than anything you could learn in a book or video. That'll make everything clear. It does not get any clearer than duck-diving or bailing your board in the biggest surf you've ever seen.

I hear so many guys saying, "Oh, that looks totally easy," but I don't think they realize the physical stress of a long tow session. It looks simple until you get out there, and the reality is you just put yourself on a 50-foot face or bigger. When I was at Todos one winter, I got like eight waves in a row, and on the ninth I got swatted, and almost drowned, because my tank was on empty. It was a simple wave, but Loya couldn't come get me because I couldn't come up. Scared the shit out of me. I was visualizing my kid, and how I needed to be back there for her, and I really thought I was going to die. Mostly because I wasn't 100 percent physically ready to take that wave.

That's when you know guys are really into it, after they've gotten a complete throttle. I've seen guys get so worked, they're just done, the mojo's over, they don't come back. And I've seen guys like Jay Moriarity, who would get totally beat and come back smiling. That's truth. That's when you know somebody's hooked, and he's out there because he loves it.

What have I learned from towing Maverick's? That the place has no size limit, and I don't think we've seen the biggest yet. Another thing is that whenever you're in doubt, pull into the barrel. I tried straightening out one time and I had the lip land right on my back leg and it rag-dolled me like no other. I still think I might have fractured a vertebrae and not known about it. I told myself to never let that happen again. I've always pulled in, no matter what, because you're way better off in the barrel than in front of it.

I guess I'm getting to be an old man, too. Not really, but I no longer feel like I have to be there for every swell, trying to take every wave. I've got a wife and child, and I've taken enough beatings to understand the consequences out there. I don't need to be at the circus every time it's open.

"Big paddle-in days work on my nerves more. You have times when you think the sky's gonna fall. Towing in, you don't understand as much what the consequences are. It doesn't seem as big as it is. The fear factor is definitely worse when you're laying down on a surfboard." — MATT AMBROSE

THE CASE FOR PADDLING

MARK RENNEKER

(Mark Renneker embodies the wilderness soul of Maverick's. He can match big-wave credentials with nearly anyone, but he takes special pleasure in the sighting of sea otters, a whale breaching outside the lineup, a slight shift in the wind, or the mere viewing of an inconceivably large wave. He could be perfectly happy without getting a single ride. On land, where he specializes in environmental concerns and alternative medicine, he is a friend and invaluable confidant to his patients. While many fellow surfers are baffled or put off by his erudite demeanor, Renneker draws universal respect. He takes a one-of-a-kind place in surfing history.)

We had an awkward conflict between tow teams and paddle surfers for several years at Maverick's. It seems that now we've reached an uneasy truce—probably because we haven't had as many giant days in recent winters—and it has relaxed the mood considerably. I still find, however, that there is no place for intrusive machinery in such a pristine setting.

Despite improvements in Jet Ski efficiency, I'm still appalled by the noise, the smell, and the sea surface disruption. Environmentally, I

PADDLING INTO GIANT WAVES IS ABOUT BEING THE
UNDERDOG— AND THAT'S PART OF THE THRILL.

PETER MEL, PADDLE-IN BARREL. TEN YEARS
LATER, THIS REMAINS A RARE SIGHT.

don't think anyone could argue that Jet Skis, or even surfboards, have no effect. If you look at biological studies, and the data presented at the Monterey Sanctuary hearings [in 2004], you'll find that marine life is affected dramatically. Common sense tells you that if you have all this racket in a small area, and you're a sea otter intending to live there and reproduce, maybe you'd think about moving up the coast to the Devil's Slide. I'm always amazed that the otters, seals, and sea lions actually persist in staying around Maverick's. It must be a very rich area for them. It couldn't be that they actually *like* all of us.

Then there's the essential difference between a paddle-surfer, out there to catch a couple of waves, and the tow-surfer, who wants thirty waves. Throughout Hawaii, a basic rule prevails: If there are paddle-surfers out, go tow somewhere else. We haven't been able to make that distinction at Maverick's. It helped that the Monterey Sanctuary hearings gave us a common guideline—no towing until the Half Moon Bay buoy reads 20 feet—but that was a suggestion, not a written rule yet.

When those 20-foot days come around, most of us understand that tow-surfers will be on it first thing in the morning. So many of those guys are all about photo opportunities, and that's their best chance to get glassy conditions in perfect light. By late afternoon, when the photographers are gone, I'm likely to find myself out there paddle-surfing with just a few friends. The problem is that in-between time, when people still want to tow. And if there's anything that bothers me more than the noise-and-stink issue, it's the *attitude* of tow-surfers when we're both out there and they're hoping we'll leave, and they're oh-so-subtly letting us know that.

We're at the peak, and there they all are, gathered around each other in the channel, revving up like Marlon Brando in *The Wild One*. It's like trying to surf with a classroom full of attention-deficit hyper-active kids. There's a prevailing impatience that precludes the incremental paddling, waiting, being content with catching just a handful of waves, feeling that the measure of the day is the whole experience. These guys are just fluttering around like a bunch of speed freaks, acting like the toughest guys around. Some days, it's like being in a crowded restaurant, and rather than people waiting by the door, they're hovering right behind your chair, taunting you to leave.

When it comes to tow-surfing preparation, it reminds me more of the Daytona Speedway than a surf spot. You have to be a good mechanic. You're castigated if your gas cap doesn't fit just right. You need to be handy with a wrench. To me, everything about the ocean is being in the water and leaving that other shit behind. I'm perfectly fine

A PADDLER'S NIGHTMARE: TOW SURFERS HOVERING ON THEIR SKIS, WAITING TO TAKE OVER.

MARK RENNEKER, WHO WOULD NEVER EVEN THINK OF TOWING, GETS HIS SHARE OF BOMBS.

MARK RENNEKER (LEFT) AND JEFF CLARK IN THE MIDDLE OF A TOW-VS.-PADDLE DEBATE.

with windsurfing, kites, canoe surfing, anything that shows human ingenuity. You lose me as soon as someone starts up an engine.

Someone asked if I ever enjoyed the sight of a surfer being towed in to a wave. At times, yes. That one session at the outer peak [in October '99], when Peter Mel really showed everyone how to do it, was remarkable. He figured it out—how far to fade, how to still make the wave—and that was an achievement. Then there was an evening a few years back when Jay Moriarity and Jeff Clark, towing together, were about the last ones left as the sun went down. Jay wasn't quite into the whole towing idea, but he rode superbly, and it was like watching an immature gazelle finally gain adult form. It was gorgeous to watch, and I loved it, because his reaction was strictly about Jay, not some photographer shooting from the channel.

I think we've learned some things from towing, as well. We know that you can take a wipeout on a 70-foot face, or have one break right on your head, and survive. Because people have been riding those waves on 6-foot tow boards, the size of our paddle boards has gone way down. Back around '96 or so, Mel had some trouble on a 9'9" and we all said, "That's it—can't go any smaller than that." But now we know you can paddle in on boards under 9 feet, or even 8 feet. Last winter, my main Mav's board was an 8-foot fish. And the best thing is that we've been able to better coexist with tow surfers lately. They've only been coming out on the really big days, when that outer peak amounts to a different surf spot than where we're sitting, closer to the channel. We don't have all these guys trying to learn how to tow-surf on the bowl, and that leaves more room for everybody.

Perhaps the most important lesson from tow-surfing is that paddle surfers should be able to go bigger, that the so-called 30-foot barrier is fictitious. We're seeing younger guys like Greg Long and Anthony Tashnick start to push those boundaries, and I think that should be the challenge. That's how the sport moves forward, when the impossible becomes reality, like the guys breaking through at Waimea Bay in the late '50s.

I don't think it takes much imagination to envision someone paddle-surfing a 30-foot wave—or bigger. If you remember where snowboarding was ten years ago, then look at what these guys are doing in Alaska—just taking straight-down, thousand-foot drops over horrifying ledges—you can see it happening. Think of what the tow guys have learned about air-dropping, riding behind the peak and being able to deal with radical situations. Take that knowledge into

GRANT WASHBURN: "It certainly makes great videos, but on average 15-to-20-foot days, seeing wave after wave attacked from behind feels wrong to me. It's one thing when the prey is a 75-foot T-rex, but some guys are felling sheep. My whole thing is being out there all the time with my friends, and they're *all* good days. I don't ever want paddle-in surfing to be some kind of letdown because of a tow-in wave I got a month ago."

KENNY COLLINS, PONDERING
WHAT MIGHT HAVE BEEN.

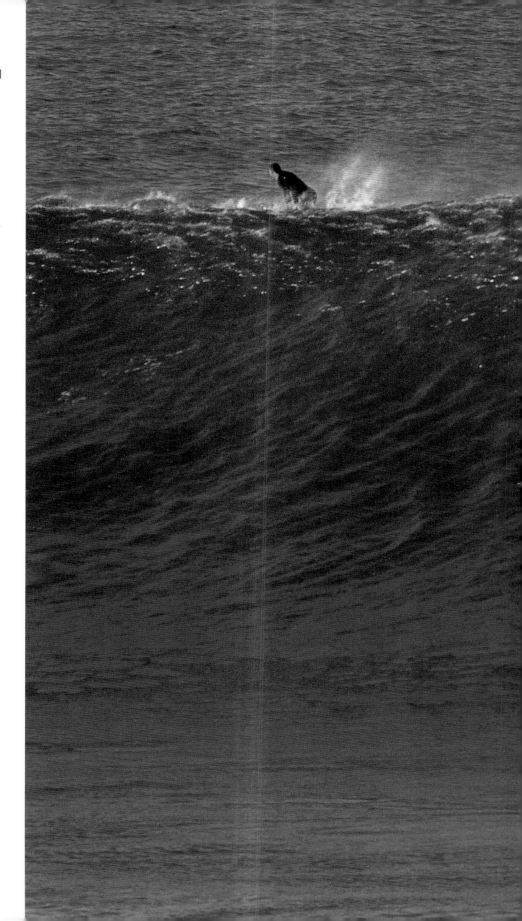

the right paddle-in day, with a little innovation in design and a God-willing sort of attitude shift—now, *that* would be a noteworthy event.

There's much to be said for looking out, seeing 30-foot waves and saying, "I'm going to find a way to paddle out there and catch one," even if it means paddling a mile out and back. Without fail, those are my favorite days of the year. It doesn't have to be the biggest wave of the day, just *any* wave. On one of those days, you've become part of the energy, the whole natural event that is taking place. It becomes a personal relationship with Maverick's, trying to surf it no matter *how* it's breaking, whether it's giant, south winds, 40-knot north winds, or just a confused morass of swell and storm. You think to yourself, how can you make the calculations, match that up with your ability, and catch at least one wave? For me, that's been the challenge from day one.

That's the best part about paddle-surfing—it's pure. It's not cheating. I've always said, give me a good water-skier from Lake Tahoe who has never set foot in the ocean, and you could have him towing big Maverick's in a day. Or you could grab a few grunge skateboarders from San Francisco, and as soon as the paint dried from the graffiti they put on the Ski, they could be towing. And, yes, you could take Condoleezza Rice and have her towing in an afternoon. If her hairstyle held up, she might even fade the bowl.

MATT AMBROSE. STAYING TRUE
TO HIS PADDLE-SURFING ROOTS.

"From the start, it was apparent Tashnick was the new kid on the block, groomed perfectly by the Santa Cruz guys. He's a straight-up kid. Real nice balance between innocence and bravado." — **DOUG ACTON**

THE PRODIGY

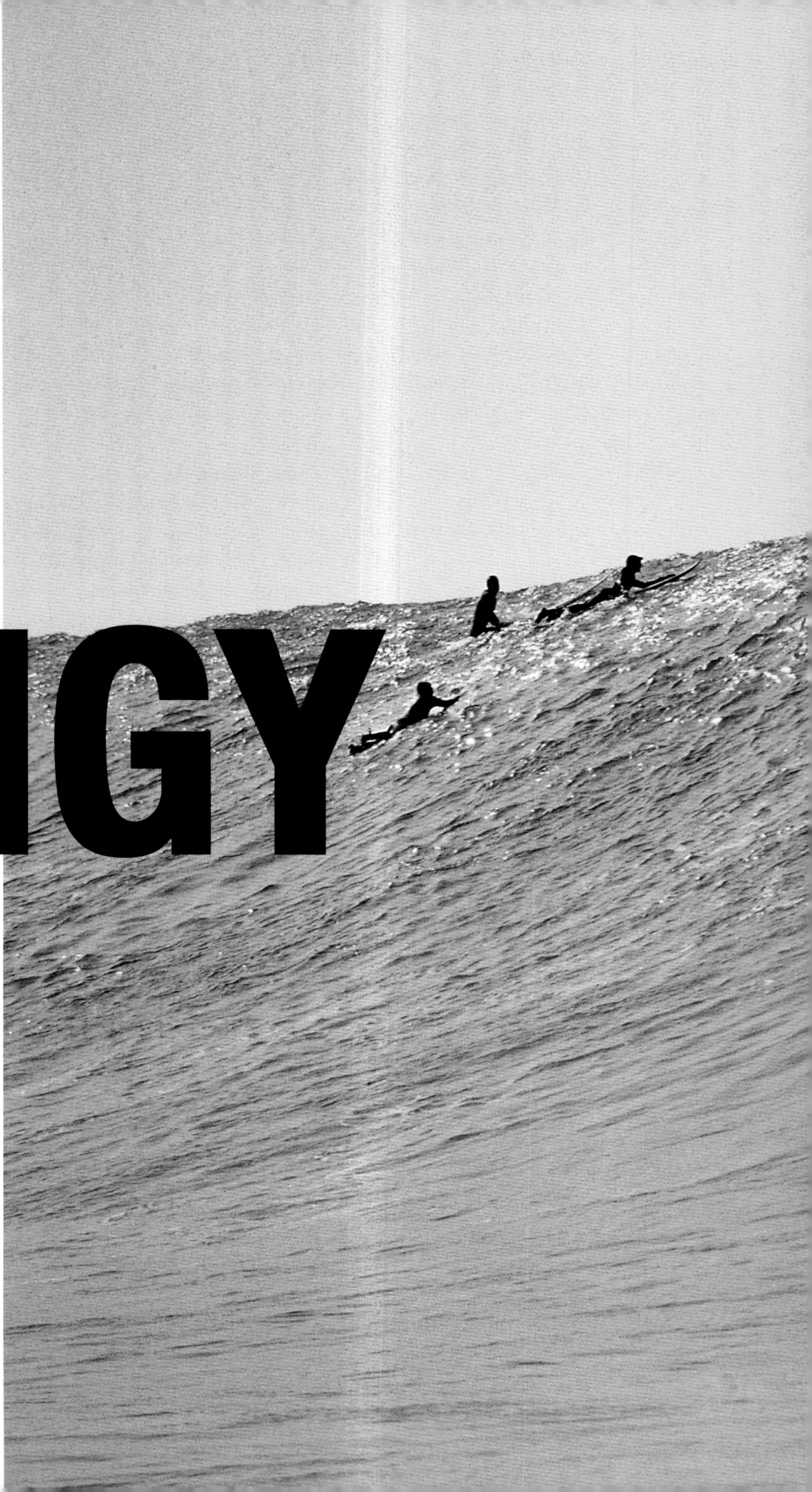

BRUCE JENKINS

The lineup at Maverick's is a haven for maturity. Big-wave surfers simply don't arrive in their mid-teens; it's an endeavor that requires experience, dues payments, and a stepladder evolution from one nasty break to the next.

And then came Anthony Tashnick.

At the age of sixteen, Tashnick attacked full-scale Maverick's in a manner distinctly reminiscent of Jay Moriarity so many years before. In January of 2001, Tashnick signaled his presence by riding the biggest paddle-in wave of that entire winter. He didn't make the wave, getting crushed after failing to generate enough speed on his bottom turn, but the mere attempt got everyone's attention.

For a while, some of the Maverick's veterans doubted Tashnick's future, figuring he had more courage than actual ability. They

ANTHONY TASHNICK'S "WAVE OF THE SEASON" IN 2001.
FROM THAT MOMENT ON, HE WAS FOR REAL.

weren't saying that in Santa Cruz, though. Tashnick is the latest in a long line of West Side surfers who have graduated from Steamer Lane, Mitchell's Cove, and Scott's Creek to Maverick's. The list includes Richard and Dave Schmidt, Vince Collier, Zach and Jake Wormhoudt, Flea and Troy Virostko, Anthony Ruffo, Peter Mel, Kenny Collins, and Josh Loya, and in the history of surfing, only the north shores of Oahu and Kauai can boast so many elite big-wave riders from a single neighborhood.

"Sometimes there's a surfer who just looks born to do it," says Mel. "Richie Schmidt was that way, and Jay Moriarity. These days, it's Tashnick. You watch him on a 4-foot day somewhere, and he surfs OK; looks kind of awkward. Then you see him on a 20-foot wave and he looks completely natural, like he's been doing it forever."

The Moriarity comparisons only go so far, whether it's style, personality, or accomplishment, and that's fine with Tashnick, who would prefer to be his own man. The most common thread between the two is desire, Tashnick having devoted his life to becoming one of the major Maverick's players. In the 2004 contest, he found himself in the final, at eighteen, with five of the best ever to surf the place: Flea, Mel, Evan Slater, Matt Ambrose, and Grant Washburn.

In the 2005 contest, Tashnick closed the deal. He not only won the event, an all-day marathon requiring as much endurance as skill, but he did so convincingly. As the victory became official at the post-contest party, it was no surprise to see him lifted upon the shoulders of Flea, Collins, and other stoked members of the West Side crew.

Since then, Tashnick has expanded his horizons. A single contest victory doesn't necessarily carry much weight among the hard-core international crowd—not when your contemporaries are Shane Dorian, Garrett McNamara, and the Irons brothers—so Tashnick has spent the last few summers on exotic surf trips, attacking serious waves around the world. The consensus opinion from every witness: He wants it, badly. This kid isn't out to prove something or just show up for appearance's sake; he takes a Flea-like mentality into the water, ready to devour every massive barrel he can find.

Looking back on his youth, Tashnick says, "I was surfing the Lane when I was twelve, as big as it would get. But I was always scared of Maverick's, like it was too gnarly. It got so hyped up after [Mark] Foo died, I told myself I wasn't even going to surf it. I procrastinated a long time, but when I turned sixteen, I figured I should try it out.

"When I first saw it, it looked like an avalanche," he says. "You know how your heart sinks when you just miss crashing into somebody head-on? I saw somebody paddle over a giant wave, and I felt that—like, holy shit, this place is for real. [Mike] Brumett told me I should sit in the channel for the first day. But when I got out there, it was kind of high tide, and I didn't really see a set, so I went straight into the bowl. Then a set came, and I was able to get one. My first couple waves were some of the best I've had out there."

From a distance, or on video, Maverick's looks like a reasonably manageable takeoff. Up close, the reality hits hard. Only the narrowest window opens for a clean entry, and just the slightest mistake sends countless riders—including some of the world's best—cascading over the falls. Tashnick mastered the Maverick's takeoff almost immediately, to the point where his smooth, apparently effortless drops are the envy of surfers around Northern California.

"It's all about confidence, and a little bit of fear," he says. "There are times when fear can psych you out, like a really bad wipeout, and then the next couple sessions you're all timid out there. But basically you want fear, because you don't want to be doing something stupid, like guys just taking off crazily with no idea what they're doing. You need fear so you won't be an idiot, but you also have to want it, so you don't hesitate and get yourself hurt."

Tashnick willingly joined the tow-in movement, but when it comes to big-wave ethics, he has an old-school mentality that wears well in the Maverick's lineup. "I'd way rather paddle in than tow," he says. "I think paddling's way gnarlier. I mean, I could whip my little brother into a Mav's wave. It takes no skill. I can't stand it when we see guys out there who never paddle in, and all of a sudden they're towing. I guess that's what some people are about, but it's wrong. It's way more fulfilling to paddle into one."

As such, Tashnick never sells himself short. While a number of Maverick's surfers are intent on riding increasingly shorter boards, Tashnick chooses the flip side. "I don't think about performance," he says. "I'm just thinking about catching the biggest possible wave I can paddle into. I'd just rather be prepared, you know? Why ride a chintzy little hot-dog board out there? I think you should ride your biggest board out there every day. Be ready when that bomb turns the horizon all black. That's the whole reason I'm out there."

KENNY COLLINS: "I knew that kid was going to be trouble the first time I saw him out there. He got blown up by a massive wave and paddled right back out. That's usually a sign of a big-wave soldier. I've seen him get so beat, and he's all, 'I love it!' That sticks in my head every time: 'I love it.'"

127

GOING LEFT

BRUCE JENKINS

In the beginning, Jeff Clark went left. Some thirty years later, the audience still cheers.

The Maverick's left gets an occasional challenge, but never in the manner that Clark unveiled in the late '70s and perfected through the spot's early popularity in the early '90s. He was alone, he didn't run from the peak, and he switched his stance. Take any photograph of Clark going left before the tow-in era, especially during large swells, and it remains the standard against which all else is measured.

There are established, respected Maverick's surfers who haven't gone left once in 20-foot surf. The consequence is just that great. It's an easy wave beyond the takeoff and bottom turn. Out on the shoulder, as the wave heads quickly toward deep water, most any capable surfer could glide safely into the channel. At the point where the lip unloads,

DOUG ACTON: "JEFF CLARK IN THE EARLY YEARS, BUSINESS AS USUAL. SURFING IT ALL BY HIMSELF, PUSHING THE LIMITS. THIS WAS AROUND '92—WE STILL HAVEN'T SEEN THE LEFT SURFED ANY BETTER."

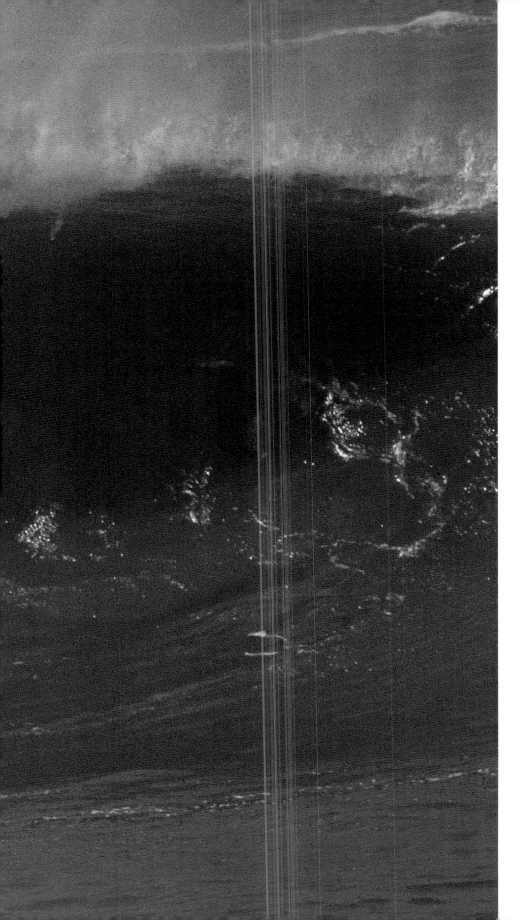

it ranks with Jaws, Teahupoo, or any other spot in the world for sheer treachery. Frighteningly thick and hollow, it invariably breaks in solitude, making for classic empty-wave shots in magazines and videos.

Clark's early performances were the product of pure innocence. Watching Maverick's from the Ross's Cove area as a kid, he thought the wave was a left. "I'd paddle out on the north side, through these gnarly closeouts—not in that nice slot where we paddle out now," he says. "I had a 7'3" single-fin, riding the lefts, and it was the fastest I'd ever gone on a surfboard. The first thing I thought was, I've got to get a bigger board. I went out and bought a 9'10", and that was the start of the Maverick's guns."

Even now, with tow-surfing crews taking over on giant days, Clark is mostly a lone warrior going left. Strapped onto his board, he no longer has the option of switching his stance, but it's remarkable to watch Clark let go of the rope, take a glance to his left, then occasionally head that way on raw instinct. "I've done it so many times before, it just seems natural to me," he says. "The thrill of it never gets old. It's a whole different rush."

Others have had success going left, notably Peter Mel, Grant Washburn, Shane Desmond, and Chris Malloy, who built on his Pipeline expertise to give it a shot. In all cases, the moments were fleeting. "The only guy to really make an impact was Kirk Young, a Hawaiian goofyfooter who paddled into some bombs in '94," says Washburn. "But nobody has surfed it consistently, like Jeff, because the risk is so heavy. When it's really big, the main left is right in the center of the pit."

"The left is just super crazy, and it hasn't been fully explored at all," says Shawn Rhodes. "That's why I say that Jeff is 'the man', because he's gotten so many huge lefts over the years. Sure, the shoulder is fat, but there's just something about it. I know some goofyfooters who should be going left all day long. For some reason, they always go right."

Without question, going left can leave surfers a bit short on glory. Most of the water photographers shoot from the channel, looking straight into the right, and no channel-bound contest judge would be able to follow someone going left. Still, the reluctance has more to do with survival than publicity.

131

"I went left a couple times," says Flea Virostko, "but I don't want to do what Clark does—fuckin' tuck under at the last second and hope your neck doesn't get torn off. I've seen him just barely get under. Could have got *so* hurt. And if you get beat on a left, you're going to be right in the zone for a northwest swell. Probably going into the rocks if there's a set."

The natural order of surfing's evolution would suggest that in time, the Maverick's left will be routinely challenged. "Of the top thousand guys in the world, I'd love to see Tom Carroll try it," says Rhodes. "Tow him in, see what he's got. See if he'll pull in. With those giant barrels, after what this guy's done at Pipeline? It would be unbelievable."

Until then, it's the last frontier. The left seems every bit as forbidding as it did in 1990, when surfers began joining Clark in the lineup. For all of his other contributions to the sport, Clark joins an exclusive list of surfers—including Jock Sutherland, Butch Van Artsdalen, and the Keaulana family (notably Buffalo and Rusty)—to regularly switch stance in serious waves.

"We owe everything to Jeff Clark, and nobody should forget that," says John Raymond, a fixture at Maverick's for years. "I'm talking about going left *or* right with nobody else out there. I don't think people understand what kind of courage that took. It's one thing for the rest of us to come in afterward, but for him to go out, at a place that looks like it just might kill you, that's unbelievable. If it wasn't for Jeff, I'll bet that place would still be cloudbreaking, and nobody would be out there."

KIRK YOUNG, 1994. STILL ONE OF THE BEST LEFTS EVER CAPTURED ON FILM.

"I hate to say it, because I do tow in, but it's true. It fucks things up and downgrades the whole spirit of big-wave paddle-surfing. Say you paddled into a 20-footer and someone else got a 25-footer towing in, and a little bit deeper. Nobody's even going to care about your wave. Maybe you and your friends realize you took the bigger chance, but who's going to know that? Nobody looking through a mag, that's for sure." — **SHAWN RHODES**

A TIME AND PLACE

ZACH WORMHOUDT

(In the grand tradition of Darrick Doerner and Gerry Lopez, the 5'9" Wormhoudt is a diminutive presence in big waves—and a powerful force. Zach and his brother, Jake, are Maverick's devotees who tend to show up an hour before daybreak and score the day's first rides. Although Zach was hit hard by the tow-in bug, he never lost his dedication to paddling. He is a two-time Maverick's contest finalist, and he won the XXL Biggest Paddle-In award for the 2003–2004 season.)

My focus has always been paddle-surfing, and it always will be. But I believe there's a place for towing, and for a lot of us, it has provided some of the greatest moments of our lives.

It's a love-hate relationship for me. Back in 1986, I was surfing Steamer Lane when a couple of guys drove by on stand-up Jet Skis. Vince Collier was sitting way outside, and he started waving his hands, flagging these guys in for help. As soon as they got close enough, Vince stood up on his board and shot it right into one of the guys. "Wake the hell up and go back to the Valley, you *kooks*!" From that day forward, that's how I looked at it: Jet Skis meant kooks

WAVES LIKE THIS CONVINCED ZACH WORMHOUDT
THAT TOWING IS A WORTHWHILE ENDEAVOR.

KENNY COLLINS: "It's just so incredible to do a big roundhouse on a huge wave. Paddle boards are just longboards in that kind of size. You can't really snap off any turns. Whereas with a 7'4" and footstraps, you're throwin' a big cutty, doing some really tight turns."

from the Valley. People without a grain of soul or the least bit of respect for the ocean. Almost twenty years later, my opinion of personal watercraft has not changed much.

My feelings wavered a bit in the mid-'90s, when the first tow-in videos started coming out of Hawaii. The best of them, *Wake-Up Call*, was exactly that. The Maui tow teams were not just catching and making giant waves, they were actually surfing them, doing turns, getting barreled. From a state of total disbelief, I immediately went out in search of my own Ski.

Now I've reached the point where I tow maybe fifteen or twenty days a year and surf the rest of the time, and I'm equally stoked on both things. There are a bunch of guys towing these days that are not really part of the big-wave paddle scene, and that's a little weird. Either they never paddled into big waves or they've given it up, yet they're anxious to tow whenever the buoys come up. That's where towing starts to get a little dicey. Most people agree that with respect to Maverick's, tow-surfing should be limited to the regular paddle-in surfers who only tow on days that are clearly too big to paddle. But what about the days when teams show up and the surf isn't as big as expected? Or the days where towing is the only way anyone is going to ride a wave, and there's a lone paddle-in guy who is going to sit on the shoulder till dark?

Am I conflicted? At times, absolutely. I just let the swells make the call. If it's too big for paddling, my brother Jake and I are ready to tow. If there's any debate whatsoever—like, maybe a few big waves can be paddled into—we won't tow. We are adamant about that. We are never going to be the tow team hovering around paddle surfers, trying to vibe them out of the lineup. Even if it's the kind of swell where you only catch one wave, the right-of-way should always go to the paddler.

I can appreciate the theory that tow teams are going to prevent guys from paddling into the next realm of big waves. I just don't think it's realistic. In fact, that is the very reason tow-in surfing came to be: inventing a way to catch and ride waves beyond the physical limits of paddle power. That's not to say the biggest paddle-in wave has

JAKE WORMHOUDT: "There's no way you can successfully tow unless you've progressed through all the stages of paddle-surfing. Once you've reached that stage, and you can afford it, it's definitely payoff time. Paddling, you're lucky to get three or four waves in an hour. With towing, you get that many in one turn, which is like fifteen minutes. With a clean pickup you can catch two waves in the same set. More waves means more time in the bowl. And that reinforces your understanding of the wave, which in turn makes you more aggressive in your surfing."

PETER MEL: "It's a good thing we've got Jet Skis to take you around, because it's not too efficient trying to paddle on a 7'4" board that's sixteen inches wide, has footstraps, and doesn't float worth a damn. Basically, it's like swimming."

NO MATTER HOW OFTEN HE TOWS, ZACH WORMHOUDT ALWAYS SHINES WHEN THE PADDLE CONTEST COMES AROUND.

already been ridden, but the boundaries are very apparent to the guys who are out there trying to paddle in. After the 25-foot mark, two things tend to happen: the waves become virtually impossible to catch via paddle power, and the surface conditions become proportionately irregular. So even if someone does manage to paddle into a 30-foot wave, the probability of making the wave is grim. For many of us the challenge is the motivation, and I will continue to try myself, but tow-in surfing is not holding back the paddle-in frontier.

If you've done much snowboarding, you understand the real lure of tow-surfing. Massive faces of water, like a big open mountain, allow you to turn and carve as much as you dare. If I were forced into a life of snowboarding exclusively, I'd be happy. That's how much I love it, and I find it remarkably similar to tow-surfing. I've done both on the same day, scurrying up to Tahoe after a morning session at Maverick's. I've set my snowboard bindings so my stance matches my tow-board setup. It's weird, too, because just as with mountain size, wave size is no longer an issue. When you're paddling in a giant, building swell, there's always the possibility that it will get too big and you'll be lucky just to make it in. With towing, the waves have never been too big—not yet, anyway. You'd think that everyone should have a cutoff point, but with towing, it doesn't seem like anyone does. Not only are the biggest waves in the world being surfed, guys are making sure they get towed into the gnarliest, most critical part.

Big-wave pioneer Peter Cole said it perfectly: "Tow-surfing misses the very essence of surfing." No part of tow-surfing provides the pure stoke of paddling into a big wave and making the drop, but still, it's an unbelievable experience. You're riding a thirty-pound board that is smaller than you and only begins to perform when it's 35 feet and choppy. You're chasing down a swell from three-quarters of a mile beyond where it will break. At that point, the swell might only look 12 feet high. It looks like nothing. Then it starts to grow—it might get to 50, 60 feet on the face—and you're thinking: What's this thing going to do when it hits the reef? Will it swing wide? Will it close out? How big is it going to get? So many dynamics come into play, but the beautiful thing is when you let go of that rope, you're free to go where your imagination takes you. You're not limited by a surfboard that is also designed for paddling; in fact, you're liberated by a board purely designed for surfing. The irony is that while it might have been relatively easy to catch that wave, you're confronted with more size than you ever imagined—and a highly dangerous situation.

Sometimes, the waves are only part of your worries. You can have a situation where your turn is up, you're being towed into a wave

from way outside, and all of a sudden, two teams on the inside flip U-turns and now they're on both sides of you, going for the same wave you waited an hour for. And they're your best friends! Oh, yeah, it's that intense. So you wonder, are they bluffing? Maybe, but we have to stake our ground. Back down once, and they'll take advantage of you all day long. That's the evil side of the tow-in dynamic, seeping in. The playing field is evened out by horsepower, while experience and ability tend to lose value.

The teamwork component can be the best thing about tow-surfing—or the worst. It's nice to have a partner, to feel the camaraderie, and that's something you don't get from paddle-surfing. Driving home together after a heavy day, that's a great feeling. But you bear a burden if things don't work out. In the worst-case scenario—someone actually dying out there—that would be a difficult hurdle to get over, and it crosses your mind every time you put somebody into a giant wave. So many times I've said to myself, "Please make that bottom turn *now*. Don't fade any more! Just make the bottom turn already!" Because you know that you're tied to the results of that ride, whether it is triumphant or tragic. Or it can put you in a position where you have to enter an incredibly dangerous situation to make a rescue.

I know that friendships have been won and lost over a partner's willingness to drive a Jet Ski into trouble, but I won't go that far. When I'm getting towed in, I'm always in paddling mode—responsible for myself only. A mistake is nobody else's fault, and if I'm screwed, I'm screwed. Sure, it's a huge relief to get rescued when you're floating in the impact zone, about to get worked, but you can never count on it. That's why the whole rescue thing is so heavy. Even when it's apparent that one must be made, sometimes the conditions are so dangerous, you have to wait. Otherwise, you're going to have two people in trouble. And that's such a fine line. Most Maverick's tow-surfers wouldn't think twice about losing a $12,000 Ski in an attempt to make a rescue. They know it's not always the best call, but they'll put their own life on the line to help someone. Rescuing each other builds a very strong bond between tow partners. It's a dynamic that people don't necessarily see, but it's a huge part of the towing experience.

The future of Maverick's tow-surfing remains uncertain. A number of surfers, adamantly opposed to the idea, are lobbying for an all-out ban of the sport within the Monterey Bay National Marine Sanctuary. In many ways, it's easy to understand and appreciate their concerns. An entire paddle session can be ruined by the rev-head attitudes of one bad-apple tow team. The pressure to leave, the noise, the wake—all combine to completely destroy the ambiance of the surfing experience.

BARNEY BARRON, RIDICULOUSLY
CALM ON A MEAN ONE.

KEN BRADSHAW: "Paddle guys are looking at 25-foot waves from the shoulder at Maverick's and just drooling. Nobody's sitting on the peak and nobody will be. The face of that wave literally scallops right out of the swell. It has more velocity, more heave, than Waimea or any other paddle-in spot. I was watching waves peel off outside of where I was sitting, and I didn't move. Better judgment told me not to."

141

The anti-tow constituency has primarily focused their arguments on issues pertaining to environmental harm, and it's certainly not hard to imagine pollution and disruption to wildlife as Jet Skis buzz in and out of the fragile coastal ecosystems. The pollution argument, however, has been substantially refuted with the recent introduction of fuel-efficient, low-emission, 4-stroke personal watercraft. There is no doubt that personal watercraft have some impacts on marine wildlife, but do the impacts warrant an all-out ban on these types of boats? How do they compare to other issues affecting wildlife in the sanctuary such as urban water runoff, the cruise ship industry, or commercial and recreational boating? Can tow-surfers acknowledge and mitigate these impacts? I believe that the most apparent problem with tow-surfing is the user conflict between paddle surfers and tow surfers. It's an issue that absolutely needs to be resolved, but who will deal with it, and how?

I would hope that we end up with tow-surfing regulations equal to or better than those recently adopted by the state of Hawaii. This entails mandatory training and licensing for people who want to tow, plus minimum surf-height requirements for the days towing would be allowed. Such regulations will not solve all the problems associated with towing, but it would be a giant step in the right direction.

I have to admit, I still hate Jet Skis. I guess it goes back to my first recollections back at Steamer Lane in '86. No matter what anyone says about towing, nothing can replace the feeling of catching a big wave on your own. Even on my most euphoric tow-in rides, I've kicked out with a certain emptiness, knowing I hadn't felt the rush of timing a big wave and making the drop. Nothing in tow-surfing compares to the pure stoke and energy of that experience, and it never will.

Sometimes, though, you get it just right. On March 9, 2005, Maverick's was bigger than it had been in five years. A dense morning fog sent most people looking for waves in Monterey and beyond. By midmorning, the fog was blown away by 20-knot northwest winds. There was no way anyone could paddle in, and yet it was epic for tow-surfing. With the takeoff issue removed, the waves were huge and smooth for the tow board. By the afternoon, Josh Loya and I were out there with just one other tow team—nobody else around. We surfed for hours and hours, picking the best wave of each set, the best set of each hour. We got so many insane waves, we lost count. Finally, we just looked at each other, sort of a quit-while-we're-ahead thing, stoked out of our minds. To me, that was perfect Maverick's. Free to surf. Free to live.

ZACH WORMHOUDT, PERENNIAL
CONTENDER FOR THE SACK AWARD.

> "He was going to be the next king of Maverick's, maybe the best big-wave rider ever, because every year he moved a step up. That next year, I think he would have won the contest—and owned it for five to ten years. He was fueling the fire, and he was going to bring his friends with him." — **KENNY COLLINS**

REMEMBERING JAY

BRUCE JENKINS

There's a tribute to him at the most jaded theater in surfing. On a railing between the Volcom compound and Gerry Lopez's old house at Pipeline, somebody plastered a sticker: Never Forget Jay Moriarity.

And they haven't. They haven't let him go. Mourning generally gives way to resignation when a loved one dies, but surfers aren't "moving on" in the wake of Jay's death five years ago. They've got him right up front in the passenger's seat.

Peter Mel was talking about Moriarity in a recent interview when he noted, for emphasis, "You know how he is." Not was. *Is.* That could be Jay on the next 25-foot bomb at Maverick's. That's Jay in the lineup, disarming the tension. That's Jay in the spirit and the soul, and if you listen closely, you might hear his goofy, distinctive laugh.

He came onto the scene so early, people couldn't quite believe what they were seeing. In a Maverick's lineup full of battle-hardened

surfers who had dedicated untold years to big-wave riding, there was Jay, a fifteen-year-old kid out of Santa Cruz, in 1993. He seemed to know nothing of life, totally naïve in his conversation and approach to other surfers, and yet he knew everything. He had studied Maverick's in the manner of a student preparing for college.

Under the tutelage of Rick "Frosty" Hesson, a long-respected mainstay of the Santa Cruz surf scene, Moriarity literally did it by the book. He studied documents prepared by Hesson on the intricacies of Maverick's. He was told to write essays, and stayed up late at night penning his thoughts. It's a classic technique—execution through visualization—but surfers aren't too fond of homework. "I was thinking, kid, that's not where it's at," Mel recalls. "Just go out there, throw yourself into the waves and deal with it. That's how you learn. But Jay did all that research and wrote everything down, and the way he went out and performed…it was almost weird."

As Frosty recalls, "At some point I realized I'd be talking about dying—really driving that point home—to someone who's fifteen years old. You wonder if you should really go there. Jay left no doubt that we should, right from his very first session at Maverick's. He was so amped, he paddled out right past Evan Slater, who somehow had got caught in the wrong spot and was struggling to get back out. And here's some fifteen-year-old kid just blowing past him. Jay got several waves that day, without hesitation. One wave, he could have floated on the strength of that big smile on his face. His eyes were just glowing. The excitement level was incredible."

By the fall of '94, Jay was in graduate school. An epic, weeklong swell arrived that December, altering the Maverick's landscape forever. It was the swell that identified heroes and pretenders, the swell that killed Mark Foo. Moriarity became an instantly historic figure when he took a death-defying wipeout, the worst anyone had ever witnessed in California, and the subsequent poster found its way into surfers' living rooms around the world. But that wasn't the story—not in Moriarity's mind. While some very accomplished surfers were

DOUG ACTON: "Jay Moriarity's first wave at Maverick's, at the age of 15, winter of 1993–94. Jay caught my attention from the beginning. It was so very clear to see where he was headed. That day he glided into a number of bombs as if he'd been doing it for years. I miss Jay. I'm so sad we didn't get to see him finish his quest."

GRANT WASHBURN: "At the end of the second contest, when we'd both been eliminated, we got completely thrashed by a wave after we'd gone inside Mushroom Rock—one of the last areas you think you'd get in trouble. It was this crazy, ridiculous thing, except Jay got held down for so long, he was *not* coming up. And then a second wave went over him. I was really worried—except it was Jay. And he came up laughing. That's why he was such a great big-wave rider. He didn't mind the ocean overpowering him."

ROBERT "WINGNUT" WEAVER: "He was very quiet and never drew attention to himself. But I traveled with the guy. You put Jay in a disco in the middle of Europe at 3 A.M., and you'll notice him right away."

FLEA VIROSTKO: "When I heard the news, I couldn't fathom Jay dying. I still can't. I'll rage, I'll party, do all kinds of crazy shit, and I'm still here. Doesn't seem fair."

sickened by the spectacle and turned away, Jay collected himself, got back on his board, and charged back into the lineup. The wipeout would not define him.

From that day on, Moriarity was a radiant, undeniable presence at Maverick's. Unfailingly cheerful and optimistic, he was the kid laughing out loud at daybreak as a thick fog and contrary winds graced a 25-foot swell. He was there in the harsh glare of a late afternoon, long after the photographers had gone home, or at dusk. It all looked excellent to Jay. He might have spent the night on the nearby cliffs, unwilling to waste any time away from his favorite break. Hawaiian surfers speak reverentially of *aloha*, a spirit that is difficult to describe but easily recognized. Jay Moriarity had that spirit. He brought kindness, generosity, and a good-hearted attitude to his every waking moment.

Moriarity was a full-blown Maverick's legend, and just barely a man, when he joined an O'Neill-sponsored crew on a surf trip to the Maldives, off the coast of India, in the summer of 2001. During a lull between swells, he engaged in a familiar practice—free-diving some 50 feet to the ocean's bottom and just hanging out there, meditating, preparing body and mind for those worst-case scenarios at Maverick's. He made a mistake that broke the first rule of diving—Do Not Go Alone—but he was Jay. Nobody gave his absence much thought. They couldn't have imagined that Moriarity, felled by a shallow-water blackout, would not return.

Without question, it was a different sort of loss in the big-wave community. Eddie Aikau was an admirably old soul when he went down trying to save the lives of his *Hokule'a* crew members in 1978, a man whose legacy was written all over the heaving peaks of Waimea Bay. Aikau may have died young, but he had *lived*. Foo was the first to admit he had few friends in life, if any. He was thoroughly detached from everyone else in the water—and on land, for that matter—and to some, that explains how his disappearance went unnoticed in a lineup more crowded than a rock concert.

Moriarity's death was so inexplicable, at such a ridiculously early age, people simply couldn't accept it. How could anyone have let Jay go diving by himself? How could his disappearance have gone unnoticed for nearly nine hours? What were they thinking? What was *Jay* thinking? It was a cold, brutal dilemma, and his close friends waged war with it for months. After a while, though, a nebulous picture became clear. James Michael Moriarity came back into focus, still twenty-two, still with us. He remains just as influential as ever at Maverick's, the standard by which all behavior and surfing performances are judged. He was one of the four or five best surfers out there *and* the best human being. That episode in the Maldives? Didn't happen. Don't even finish the story. There is no "was."

"Oh, he's absolutely still here," says Grant Washburn. "I think about him constantly—what it meant to have him in the lineup, what it *still* means. I've got this T-shirt that says JAY across the front, so I take him wherever I go. Fiji, South Africa—Jay had a pretty good summer."

Jeff Clark remains at the forefront of denial, because he still hears the laughter. "I keep remembering this one giant wave when I was paddling, then pulled back because I saw Jay taking off on the inside," says Clark. "Watching him from behind, just for a second I saw his face and I could hear him cackling. He was weightless, just freefalling down the face, but in control, and that's how he looked at it—laughing."

Nobody understood Jay's progression better than Clark, because they were tow-in partners for some of the biggest, cleanest swells ever seen at Maverick's. They were out there at dawn, and as the sun went down. They took on the fearsome west swells when the current runs south to north, straight to hell. They pulled into barrels on 50-foot faces; they took off on *anything*. It was the master and the protégé in perfect harmony, two men with little in common yet everything they needed.

A few souls were lucky to witness their act on the evening of January 19, 2001, trading giant waves in relative solitude. "We used the light of the harbor to get in that night," says Clark, his mind fixed on Jay's signature ride: cascading to the bottom with arms at his side, styling off the bottom like some casual longboarder at Malibu, taking the risky high line, then pulling into a massive barrel and—so rare at Maverick's—coming out. Watching a wave that "looked like death," in Mike Gerhardt's words, a handful of people were screaming in the channel, their minds fully blown. "Too dark to document," says Clark. "But we've got it in our minds."

Knowing Jay, he probably talked about one of Clark's waves that night. He seemed to take great pleasure in the next person's accomplishments. On a memorable afternoon in March of '99, when Dan Moore (towed in by Ken Bradshaw) caught the biggest Maverick's wave ever ridden at the time, Moore was overcome by humility when he got back to the launching spot. He wasn't ready to call it anything great. It took the childlike exuberance of Moriarity, who had watched from the cliff, to bring the point home. Shouting, laughing, all but shaking Moore by the shoulders, Moriarity celebrated that wave as if it were his own.

Most big-wave surfers tend to be somewhat intimidating, in a variety of ways. One look at Laird Hamilton's intense, darting eyes, and a young surfer wouldn't have the first clue what to say to him. Darrick Doerner exudes heaviness and mystery, completely in a world of his own. To meet Roger Erickson is to see a man haunted by the gravity of his accomplishments. They're all decent guys, as it turns out, but Jay was more approachable than an encyclopedia salesman. He felt that you were the most important guy around, and he made certain to remember your name. "He was so nice when I first met him, I thought he was fake," says Matt Ambrose. "I thought it was an act, to get himself into Maverick's and be one of the boys. After a while, you start going, 'This guy's for real.' That rubbed off on everybody."

Mel remembers Jay from the early days in Santa Cruz, when the kid took his act out to Pleasure Point. "I'm checking him out, you know, always smiling, joy, happiness, wouldn't hurt a fly—that bugged the shit out of me," says Mel, laughing. "Just this totally naïve kid, paddling inside of you, trying not to do anything wrong, that just bugged me so much. He's all, 'Hi! How ya doin'?' And I'm like, fuck, this kid *again*? What I learned is that I judged him before I'd ever spoken to him. I should embrace somebody like that, not keep him at arm's length. Now that he's gone, I'd never do that again to somebody. I'm a nicer, more mature person because of Jay."

"I knew that kid was a piece of sunshine," says Ken "Skindog" Collins, another longtime friend from Santa Cruz. "He had sun in his eyes. Such a nice guy, but such a badass at the same time—pretty rad combo. He was definitely going to be the king of Mav's, that's for sure. He was getting good at tow surfing, and he was already one of the best paddle surfers, hands down. He would have pushed us all up a notch. I think he would have been one of the world's greatest."

Richard Schmidt saw a lot of himself when he watched the kid surf. Many years before, Schmidt had been the up-and-coming star from Santa Cruz, making pilgrimages to Hawaii (as Moriarity did) to test his mettle. And yet, Schmidt struggles for comparisons. "Jay changed a lot of people's perspectives," he says. "Here was a young guy with all the talent in the world, but no attitude. A lot of young surfers might have Jay's ability, and they're great athletes and all that, but they look down on people who aren't as good. Jay wasn't like that. He'd look straight across at you, no matter who you were,

with a smile on his face. Everybody who spent time around him was affected by that.

"Watching the footage of him surfing the year before he died, I thought he was on a level of his own," says Schmidt. "It was amazing to me. He was at the pinnacle of his surfing when he passed on. That's etched in my memory. Those images of him on his red board . . . just flying! And you could tell he had a big grin on his face. So at home in such a heavy place."

Shawn Rhodes, accustomed to the usual jockeying and hassling in killer surf, couldn't get over Jay's presence in the Maverick's lineup. "It always amazed me how he'd ask for people in the lineup. Like, where's Ambrose? Where's Grant? So opposite from the whole competitive thing. Usually if someone's not around, you're thinking, hey, I'm one-up on him. But Jay really missed having them out there. That taught me something. Surfing isn't about competing with the next guy, or getting the shot, or making the contest. It's about having fun with everyone and keeping that friendship going in the water. I'd forgotten that."

It's so fitting that Moriarity was equally at home on a minuscule tow board or a 10-footer for paddle-in sessions. Such an approach requires balance, a futuristic bent with a nod to the past, an ability to see both sides of an argument. Some of the very best at Maverick's—Mel, Flea Virostko, Shawn Barron—have found it difficult to paddle-surf there after getting a taste of massive tow-ins. Washburn won't even hear of towing, for fear he'll become addicted. Mark Renneker would rather paddle into 30-foot surf, and just marvel at the spectacle, than stoop to riding behind a Jet Ski. Somehow, Moriarity existed comfortably in both camps. He was also a world-class longboarder in smaller surf. He wanted a taste of everything, always with exceptional results.

"My best memories are from the early years, right around Jay's second season at Maverick's," says Rhodes. "There was one really low-tide day, maybe 12 to 15 feet, not real big but glassy and clean, and it was just five of us out there, including Jay. For five solid hours, we traded waves. It seemed like every time a set would come, it would be five waves, one for all of us. Then right back out to the peak, all stoked and talking about it. Nobody else out, nobody taking pictures, not even anyone on the cliff. Just a soul crew and a soul session. You don't get that anymore."

Now that he's gone, says Rhodes, "It's kind of a reality check. It could be you or me, and it could be tomorrow. So don't get too

JAY MORIARITY TAKING ONE OF HIS COUNTLESS
DROPS DURING THE DECEMBER '94 SWELL.

ESSENTIAL JAY MORIARITY (LEFT, WITH JEFF CLARK):
CELEBRATING SOMEONE ELSE'S GLORY.

RICHARD SCHMIDT: "It's kind of ironic that he spoke of me as an inspiration. When I look back on the way he was—take life for what it is, don't hold back, share with your friends—he's my greatest inspiration."

RICK "FROSTY" HESSON: "It's easy to be a hero, for a moment. It's much more difficult to be a hero in all your actions, every day. Jay chose to be a hero every day."

MIKE GERHARDT: "At the Pleasure Point memorial, more than a thousand people were in the water. After all the yelling and splashing of water, it went dead silent for minutes. All you could hear was nature. It was an intense, spiritual experience. We felt Jay was going back to the ocean, where he belongs."

caught up with your work, your mortgage, whatever else might stress you out. I have a good group of friends, but I don't think any of them quite have Jay's attitude. One time I was out in the lineup with Ambrose, talking about some job where a guy screwed someone over, and we're all bitter and serious. Jay paddles right up to us, like, 'What are you guys *talking* about?' We just started laughing. Let's forget that shit and go get some waves."

So they get their waves, and they think about Jay, and when the waves vanish for the summer, the kid sticks around. "I think about him a lot in the off-season, how hard he used to prepare," says Collins. "We were all at some trade show in the middle of summer one time, and we started talking about Maverick's, and he drops and pumps out 100 push-ups. I'm like, dude, aren't you embarrassed, people are looking at us. He's just, boom-boom-boom! *So* amped. I think about him every time I surf, too. He's there in spirit, just like all the great ones who died in their prime. He'll be a James Dean, always remembered that way. He's always going to be that smiling, sunshine kid."

On the day of Jay's memorial, when a huge group of surfers paddled out for a Maverick's ceremony, there wasn't much surf. "It was flat," Rhodes recalls. And yet...

"We're all sitting there talking, and all of a sudden there's this giant set," says Rhodes. "I'm like, oh my God, no leash, I can't believe this. I tried to duck-dive it, but somebody bailed his longboard right over me and I had to let my board go. Sure enough, right into the rocks. Broken fin. Happened to Jim Tjogas and Mike Gerhardt, too. That was strictly from Jay, right there. He had a good laugh on that one."

That's just how he is.

THE BIGGEST SWELLS

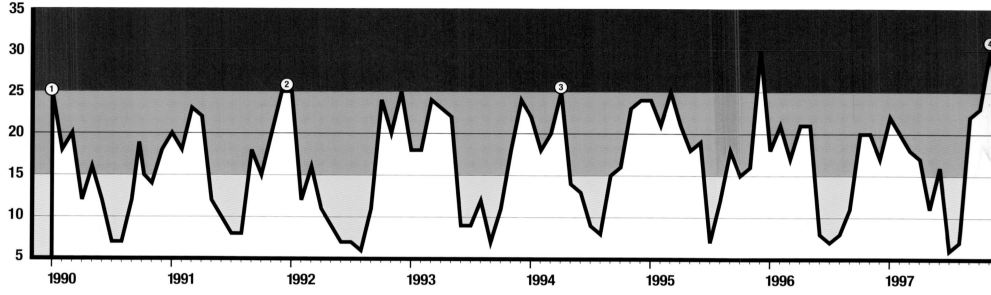

| | 1990 | 1991 | 1992 | 1993 | 1994 | 1995 | 1996 | 1997 |

When harbors start closing out and piers are in jeopardy, Maverick's comes alive. Here is a chart of the biggest swells taken from my daily calendar, along with some highlights from the past fifteen years and comments from the crew.

1. 1/12/90 Coming-Out Party: Jeff Clark runs into Santa Cruz chargers Dave "Big Bird" Schmidt and Tom Powers, along with San Francisco legend Doc "Hazard" Renneker, at Ocean Beach. They are inspecting a huge, unruly swell. Doc dives into the madness, but Jeff lures Dave and Tom down to his mysterious break. The historic session they enjoyed would send shock waves through the surfing world and forever alter big-wave riding.

2. 1/29/92 The Real Super Bowl: Doc drags his wide-eyed neighbor, Grant Washburn, down for his first session. Richard Schmidt, back from Hawaii, scratches into a 25-foot monster that swallows him whole, spits him onto O'Neill garment tags all over the world, and gives the impressionable Washburn an image he will never shake. (pp. 12, 22, 122, 130)

3. 12/18–23/1994 The Week of the Peak: An incredible string of weather systems lines up across the Pacific. Surfers revel in the phenomenal quantity. After a dozen magical Maverick's sessions, the streak comes to a tragic end with the drowning of Mark Foo. (pp. 46, 48, 54, 78, 80, 82, 84, 88, 118, 119, 132, 151, 158)

> *"It was the swell of a lifetime, maybe the greatest Northern California swell ever. For 11 days it stayed up between 10 and 20 feet, even bigger, and for almost all that time it was smooth and clean."* —Mark Renneker

> *"I don't think I'd want it any bigger. There were waves that nobody wanted any part of. That Monday, when it was blowing so hard offshore, I was thinking, 'Man will not be able to conquer this.' It was so beyond anything I'd ever experienced."* —Evan Slater

4. 1/30/98 Big Friday: El Niño churns up typhoons, mudslides, and huge surf, raging nearly all month. On this frightening 30-foot day with offshore winds, Neil Matthies is held underwater nearly 50 seconds on his two-wave hold-down. (pp. 68, 72, 96, 120)

> *"It was like, way beyond. All windy and heaving. Pretty gnar-gnar."* —Kenny Collins

> *"I had just gotten up to the cliff when I heard people screaming, freaking out. I looked up and saw that second wave, and the one behind it, hey . . . we thought we had a dead guy here. I talked to Neil later. He just kept saying, 'I saw God, man.' Over and over."* —John Raymond

> *"People seem to think it's easy paddling out at Maverick's. Not on a giant day. It's like a living hell. I watched Peter Mel try to paddle out twice and get turned back. I got dragged all the way down to Blackhand, and when I got out there, I got caught inside a 25-footer. I was down so long, my inner consciousness just turned off. My scorecard for the day: Six hours, two waves."* —Don Curry

> *"Everybody said, 'I can't believe you're alive.' I feel the same way after watching the video. That was crazy. Down there, pain has nothing to do with it. It's just your will."* —Neil Matthies

5. 11/24/98 Serious Turkey: Large mid-period swells light up the coast. Ken Bradshaw pays the locals a visit, and is treated to a roaring show of Maverick's madness. He shares a bit of his newly acquired tow-in knowledge. (p. 91)

6. 2/28/99 Heavy West: Evan Slater blows out his knee on this menacing beast of a swell. One of the days where Maverick's is meaner than it looks, and it looks plenty mean. (p. 138)

7. 10/28/99 The Outer Realm: Biggest day of the decade. A 53-foot, 17-second reading on the outer buoy stuns local surfers. Everyone anticipates a swell for the ages, and Maverick's does not disappoint. (pp. 28, 98, 102, 108, 136)

> *"Here it is the first day of the season, and we're looking at 60-foot faces. It was like going from 0 to 200 miles an hour without warning. I can't ever remember feeling that skittish out there."* —Jeff Clark

> *"Pete and I figured we'd show up and there'd be a half-dozen crews with skis and tow ropes. And then . . . nothing. The first hour, we got waves that nobody even saw."* —Kenny Collins

BY GRANT WASHBURN

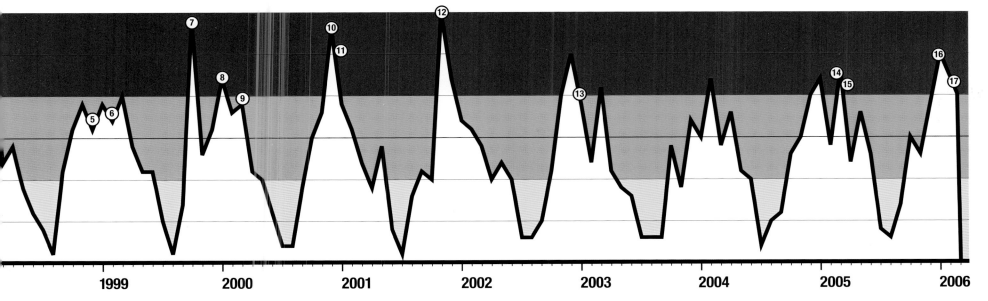

1999   2000   2001   2002   2003   2004   2005   2006

8. 2/2/00 The Revolution Is Televised: Another massive swell allows the crew to tune their acts and push new boundaries. Cameras multiply. (pp. 101, 104, 134, 142)

9. 3/3/00 The BIG Event: Contest day, with a 25-foot rogue swell challenging the finest chargers available. The videos might be as shocking and spectacular as anything seen in paddle-surfing. Jay Moriarity gets robbed when the judges place Kelly Slater ahead of him in the semis. Flea wins the title. Maverick's wins the day. (pp. 43, 44, 86, 94, 157)

"It was the biggest contestable surf ever. Even at Waimea, on the big bombs, there's someone on the peak and he's going. At real Maverick's, you go beyond that. When the real bombs came through, we all had to back off. But in the end, we felt that the performance level jacked up a notch." —Jeff Clark

"Kelly Slater really stepped up today, but he was out of the bowl. He was sittin' a lot farther over. Took a safe route. Flea didn't. That was the difference." —Kenny Collins

"There's nothing like the drama of a guy sitting, turning, taking a few strokes and paddling in during those few delicate seconds, just hangin' by a thread. Today I saw guys going off in truly heinous conditions—the best surfing I've ever seen in my life." —Steve Dwyer

10. 12/22/00 Outer Realm Reprise: One of the biggest days yet, and it's clean. Sets a solid 30 feet, sometimes bigger, greeted by four or five tow teams of really skilled riders: Schmidt, Pete, Ross, Flea, Jeff, Jay, the Wormhoudts—and they all want the biggest wave. Flea has that straighten-out bomb, just the heaviest thing imaginable, and then here comes Noah [Johnson] on a wave that looks 75 feet tall and is peeling like a point break. (pp. 32, 64, 152)

"Flea's wave gives me nightmares to this day. Josh Loya was nice enough to tow him in, and Flea was crazy enough to fade halfway to San Francisco. Definitely the heaviest wave since Laird's at Teahupoo." —Evan Slater

11. 1/19/01 New Kid on the Block: Giant swells combine with perfect conditions to create a magical Maverick's day, absolutely perfect from 9 A.M. to sunset. Several monstrous waves are ridden, and a Santa Cruz hellgrom named Anthony Tashnick glides into the scene. (pp. 2, 30, 40, 116, 124, 127, 128)

12. 11/21/01 Big Fall: Maverick's surfers gather for the first significant swell to arrive after the passing of Jay Moriarity, and the day is dedicated to him. It's the biggest swell we've ever seen out there, tormented by rain and foul winds, but offering up 75, maybe even 85-foot faces. Even the tow teams are shamelessly shoulder-hopping. And after the last team departs, a 100-foot set allegedly roars down the coast. (pp. 76, 106, 140)

"Hands-down the biggest Mav's day ever. And just nonstop. Brock Little said there are no limits to tow-surfing, but I'm not so sure now." —Kenny Collins

13. 1/1/03 Happy New Year: A massive swell hits as the ball drops in Times Square. Early birds score uncrowded perfection as 2003 begins with a bang! (p. 62)

14. 3/2/05 The 4th Maverick's Event: Tazzy takes the title in solid surf. Shane Desmond catches the wave of the year, and Mike Brumett wins the high-dive award for his three-story doughnut. (p. 52)

15. 3/9/05 The Fog: Obscured by a dense marine layer, amped riders push limits in low visibility. Ghost Trees shines in the sun, but some of the biggest waves of the year are ridden without notice on the outer bowl at Maverick's.

16. 1/4/06 The Sun: In the kind of perfect conditions that rarely come along, 30-foot, 20-second energy roars into the point and just a few elite tow teams are on it. Incredible displays of barrel riding and progressive small-wave maneuvers make a stunning session even more spectacular. Paddle surfers score a window of miraculous pits before offshore winds ruin their parade.

17. 2/7/06 Twiggy Time: South Africa's Grant "Twiggy" Baker wins the 5th annual Maverick's bombfest in ideal conditions. Brock Little smiles through numerous caves on a day he calls "one of the best of my surfing career." (pp. 18, 50)

JEFF CLARK, EARLY-MORNING STOKE

THE OLD ROADHOUSE CAFÉ, 1998

GENTLEMEN WHO RIDE MOUNTAINS

RICHARD SCHMIDT AND THE WORMHOODT BROTHERS

CEREMONIAL PADDLE-OUT AT THE
JAY MORIARITY TRIBUTE, 2001

GRANT WASHBURN

ION BANNER DROP, 2000 CONTEST

RICHARD SCHMIDT, ROSS CLARKE-JONES, AND DON CURRY BEFORE THE CONTEST, 2001

PETER MEL INDULGES THE MEDIA

DON CURRY FUELING UP

VINCE COLLIER AND THE BOYS ON THE DOCK, 1999 CONTEST

HERMAN FRISCO

THE MOHAWK GANG, WITH RINGLEADER ZACH WORMHOUDT (FAR RIGHT)

JAY AND FROSTY: FIELD TRIP

LEGENDARY ROGER ERICKSON
WITH JEFF CLARK, 2003

RICHARD SCHMIDT, SHANE DESMOND, AND FLEA VIROSTKO

UNDERGROUND CHARGER JON BANNER

CHRIS MALLOY, 1994

JAKE WORMHOUDT

ZACH WORMHOUDT, FLEA, KELLY SLATER, TONY RAY, AND QUIKSILVER'S BOB McKNIGHT AT THE 2000 CONTEST CEREMONY

FLEA AND TAZZY, WITH VICTORY IN COMMON

LATE AFTERNOON

YOUNG GUNS OF '94: JAY MORIARITY AND EVAN SLATER

PILLAR POINT HARBOR

Breakwater Constructed by
U.S. ARMY
CORPS OF ENGINEERS
SAN FRANCISCO DISTRICT
Sponsored by
SAN MATEO COUNTY
HARBOR COMMISSION

PRIDE OF PACIFICA: AMBROSE AND RHODES